TEACHERS AS ARCHITECTS OF LEARNING

SECOND EDITION

Twelve Constructs to
Design and Configure Successful
Learning Experiences

GAVIN GRIFT

CLARE MAJOR

FOREWORD BY JANELLE WILLS

Solution Tree | Press

a division of
Solution Tree

American version published in the United States by Solution Tree Press

555 North Morton Street
Bloomington, IN 47404
800.733.6786 (toll free) / 812.336.7700
FAX: 812.336.7790

email: info@SolutionTree.com
SolutionTree.com

Visit **go.SolutionTree.com/instruction** to download the free reproducibles in this book.

Printed in the United States of America

Library of Congress Cataloging-in-Publication Data

Names: Grift, Gavin, author. | Major, Clare, author.
Title: Teachers as architects of learning : twelve constructs to design and
   configure successful learning experiences / Gavin Grift, Clare Major.
Description: Second edition. | Bloomington : Solution Tree Press, [2020] |
   Includes bibliographical references and index.
Identifiers: LCCN 2020009897 (print) | LCCN 2020009898 (ebook) | ISBN
   9781951075392 (paperback) | ISBN 9781951075408 (ebook)
Subjects: LCSH: Learning, Psychology of. | Learning strategies. | Effective
   teaching. | Active learning.
Classification: LCC LB1060 .G745 2020 (print) | LCC LB1060 (ebook) | DDC
   370.15/23--dc23
LC record available at https://lccn.loc.gov/2020009897
LC ebook record available at https://lccn.loc.gov/2020009898

Solution Tree
Jeffrey C. Jones, CEO
Edmund M. Ackerman, President

Solution Tree Press
President and Publisher: Douglas M. Rife
Associate Publisher: Sarah Payne-Mills
Art Director: Rian Anderson
Managing Production Editor: Kendra Slayton
Production Editor: Rita Carlberg
Content Development Specialist: Amy Rubenstein
Text and Cover Designer: Abigail Bowen
Editorial Assistants: Sarah Ludwig and Elijah Oates

Teachers as Architects of Learning: Twelve Constructs to Design and Configure Successful Learning Experiences
(2nd ed.) originally published in Australia by Hawker Brownlow Education

© 2018 by Hawker Brownlow Education

This book is dedicated to the memory of my father,
Gert Grift, who taught me so much.

—Gavin Grift

Illustration by Gert Grift

Acknowledgments

We wrote *Teachers as Architects of Learning* (2nd ed.) to offer further support to educators—those in the business of providing opportunities for others to be successful. We were able to complete this task with the encouragement of our family, friends, and colleagues. We thank those people for their influence, thoughts, passion, professionalism, and support.

It would be remiss of us not to single out the following people for their significant influences on our thinking in the development of this second edition of *Teachers as Architects of Learning*. They include but are not limited to Hawker Brownlow Education, in particular Elaine Brownlow for her unwavering support; Solution Tree Press, for such thorough editing support; Thinking Collaborative, in particular Doreen Miori-Merola and Carolee Hayes, whose work continues to influence and inspire; Nancy McNally, a talented colleague, strong advocate, and shining light; Colin Sloper, a long-term educational guide on the side; and Dr. Janelle Wills, whose deep and high-level thinking helped to inspire this second edition.

There are also countless educators through the course of their work with us who have continued to shape, refine, and further our understanding of what the content and intended outcomes for this second edition might need to be. Their feedback has been instrumental in making the changes to both the structure and content of the book, especially those who have engaged in the Teachers as Architects workshops, institutes, and coaching sessions.

Finally, to our own children, who were and are the motivation for persevering. We are driven to continue the pursuit for excellence in our profession so children like ours reap the rewards.

Solution Tree Press would like to thank the following reviewers:

Danielle Bennett
Mathematics Teacher
Fossil Ridge Intermediate School
Saint George, Utah

Carol Watson
Fifth-Grade Teacher
Vallecitos School District
Fallbrook, California

Karen Krantz
Sixth-Grade Teacher
Adams Elementary School
Spokane, Washington

Molly Weber
Fourth-Grade Teacher
Mountain Meadow Elementary School
Buckley, Washington

Table of Contents

About the Authors...xiii

Foreword...xv

Chapter 1 — Introduction..1

    Focusing on the Learning 2

    The Key to Change: Some Promising Research.................................5

        Professional Learning Communities 5

        Teaching for Understanding 6

        The New Art and Science of Teaching..6

        Formative Assessment...7

        Productive Habits of the Mind 8

        Connections to Learning Theory 9

    The Building of Teaching Wisdom 12

    The *Teachers as Architects of Learning* Mission.................................13

        To Activate Successful Student Learning.....................................14

        To Grow in Consciousness About How Intentional Teaching Practices Impact Successful Learning 15

        To Learn Through Reflection Both on and in Action 16

    The Twelve Constructs Defined 17

    The Twelve Constructs for a Successful Learning Experience.............18

    How to Use This Book 23

    How This Book Is Structured 25

    Conclusion...26

Chapter 2 — Questioning..27

    Rationale 27

    Questioning Strategies to Consider..28

    Putting the Learning in Context: Sample Scenarios............................31

        Scenario One...31

        Scenario Two...31

    When Effective Questioning Is Missing...32

    When Effective Questioning Is Evident 33

Think and Reflect 34

Supporting Ideas and Research 34

Chapter 3—Self-Assessment: Reflection and Feedback 35

Rationale 35

Self-Assessment Strategies to Consider 38

Learning Continuums 39

Learning Maps 40

Reflections 40

Putting the Learning in Context: Sample Scenarios 42

Scenario One 42

Scenario Two 43

When Self-Assessment Is Missing 44

When Self-Assessment Is Evident 44

Think and Reflect 45

Supporting Ideas and Research 45

Chapter 4—Observing and Listening 47

Rationale 47

Observing and Listening Strategies to Consider 48

Putting the Learning in Context: Sample Scenarios 49

Scenario One 50

Scenario Two 50

When Observing and Listening Are Missing 51

When Observing and Listening Are Evident 51

Think and Reflect 52

Supporting Ideas and Research 52

Chapter 5—Explicit Instruction 55

Rationale 55

Explicit Instruction Strategies to Consider 56

Putting the Learning in Context: Sample Scenarios 57

Scenario One 57

Scenario Two 58

When Explicit Instruction Is Missing 59

When Explicit Instruction Is Evident 59

Think and Reflect 60

Supporting Ideas and Research 60

Chapter 6—Modeling and Exemplars 61

Rationale 61

Modeling and Exemplar Strategies to Consider 62

Putting the Learning in Context: Sample Scenarios 63

    Scenario One: Professor Hart's Class 64

    Scenario Two: Dr. Pure's Class 64

When Modeling and Exemplars Are Missing 65

When Modeling and Exemplars Are Evident 65

Think and Reflect 66

Supporting Ideas and Research 66

Chapter 7—Support and Safety 67

Rationale 67

Support and Safety Strategies to Consider 69

    Cognitive Learning Support 69

    Behavioral Learning Support 70

    Structural Support 70

Putting the Learning in Context: Sample Scenarios 72

    Scenario One 72

    Scenario Two 72

When Support and Safety Are Missing 74

When Support and Safety Are Evident 74

Think and Reflect 75

Supporting Ideas and Research 75

Chapter 8—Time 77

Rationale 77

Time Strategies to Consider 79

Putting the Learning in Context: Sample Scenarios 81

    Scenario One 81

    Scenario Two 81

When Consideration of Time Is Missing 82

When Consideration of Time Is Evident 83

Think and Reflect 83

Supporting Ideas and Research 84

Chapter 9—Expectation 85

Rationale 85

Expectation Strategies to Consider 87

Putting the Learning in Context: Sample Scenarios 88

    Scenario One...88

    Scenario Two 89

When Expectations Are Missing 89

When Expectations Are Evident 90

Think and Reflect 91

Supporting Ideas and Research 91

Chapter 10—Lifeworlds...93

Rationale 93

Lifeworld Connection Strategies to Consider...94

Putting the Learning in Context: Sample Scenarios 95

    Scenario One...95

    Scenario Two 96

When Connections to Lifeworlds Are Missing 97

When Connections to Lifeworlds Are Evident 97

Think and Reflect 98

Supporting Ideas and Research 98

Chapter 11—Desire...99

Rationale 99

Desire-Generating Strategies to Consider..100

    Finding an Authentic Audience for Student Learning 101

Putting the Learning in Context: Sample Scenarios 103

    Scenario One...103

    Scenario Two 103

When Desire Is Missing..104

When Desire Is Evident 105

Think and Reflect 106

Supporting Ideas and Research 106

Chapter 12—Resources 109

    Rationale 109

    Resource Strategies to Consider 110

    Putting the Learning in Context: Sample Scenarios 111

        Scenario One 112

        Scenario Two 112

    When Resources Are Missing 113

    When Resources Are Evident 114

    Think and Reflect 115

    Supporting Ideas and Research 115

Chapter 13—Existing Knowledge 117

    Rationale 117

    Strategies to Consider for Determining Existing Knowledge 118

    Putting the Learning in Context: Sample Scenarios 119

        Scenario One 119

        Scenario Two 120

    When Consideration of Existing Knowledge Is Missing 120

    When Consideration of Existing Knowledge Is Evident 121

    Think and Reflect 122

    Supporting Ideas and Research 122

Appendix 123

References and Resources 141

Index 151

About the Authors

Gavin Grift

Gavin Grift is the founder and CEO of Grift Education. Gavin's passion, commitment, humor, and highly engaging style have made him an in-demand presenter of keynotes and seminars. As a speaker, Gavin connects with international audiences on how to cultivate authentic collaboration, build success in others, and genuinely commit to reflective practice. His belief in the development of defined professional autonomy for educators challenges and connects the heads and hearts of his audience members.

Gavin has held numerous educational leadership positions, including serving as a cluster educator, leading teacher, assistant principal, director of professional learning, and executive director and managing director of Hawker Brownlow Education and Solution Tree Australia.

Gavin serves as a training associate for Thinking Collaborative's Cognitive Coaching Seminars® and PLCs at Work®. Gavin is the cofounder of the Centre of Learning Architects, in support of both teachers and leaders becoming students of their own professional practice.

He is coauthor of numerous articles and books, including *Collaborative Teams That Transform Schools and Transformative Collaboration*, and he revised *Learning by Doing* with Colin Sloper for an Australian context. He led the development of PLC networks across Australian schools, culminating in the establishment of the Centre for Professional Learning Communities. He is committed to growing the legacy of Richard and Rebecca DuFour's work through the PLC at Work® process. To learn more about Gavin's work, visit www.grifteducation.com.

Clare Major

Clare Major is the founder and CEO of Clinical Psychology Australia. She has worked within public and independent school systems for more than twenty years. In this time, her roles have included classroom teacher, student welfare coordinator, regional project leader, and principal. Clare is the cofounder of the Centre of Learning Architects.

Clare's knowledge and expertise have informed educational policy. As a master educator and clinical psychologist, Clare challenges the status quo, examining the fundamentals of leading and learning. This has led her to working with corporate organizations, educational institutions, and private practices. Her work with the University of Melbourne has included teaching within psychology and medical faculties in the areas of developmental child psychology, general psychopathology, and neuropsychology.

Clare is a published academic author of peer-reviewed journal articles on neuropsychology and developmental psychology. Her passion centers on understanding the link between brain, behavior, and the role of emotions. To learn more about Clare's work, visit www.grifteducation.com.

To book Gavin Grift or Clare Major for professional development, contact pd@SolutionTree.com.

Foreword

The research is clear, confirming unequivocally the crucial role that teachers have in improving student learning. But as Dinham, Ingvarson, and Kleinhenz (2008) point out, "The major challenge in improving teaching lies not so much in identifying and describing quality teaching, but in developing structures and approaches that ensure widespread use of successful teaching practices: to make best practice, common practice" (p.14).

The most successful teachers are never satisfied with what they know as they face the new challenges that each new year delivers. Highly effective teachers are first and foremost learners who are in continual pursuit of knowledge, evidence-informed processes, and strategies known to improve learning. They question their practices—the what, the how, and the why of their approaches. In other words, they are reflective.

Reflective practice is critical to the development of expertise (Marzano, 2012). This notion is not new. Indeed, as early as 1987, Schön highlighted that what sets skilled practitioners apart from their peers is their ability to reflect in action, thus increasing their tacit knowledge and consequently their pedagogical skill. Ericsson, Krampe, and Tesch-Römer (1993) took this concept one step further and pointed out that the development of expertise is a product of deliberate practice. Individuals engaged in deliberate practice strive to achieve mastery of "increasingly higher levels of performance through the acquisition of more complex and refined cognitive mechanisms" (Ericsson, Roring, & Nandagopal, 2007, p. 24). But what exactly are teachers to be deliberate about? *Teachers as Architects of Learning* provides the answer! Giving very clear, evidence-based, and practical advice for teachers wishing to explore specific areas for deliberate practice.

Like no other book, *Teachers as Architects of Learning* provides the structures and metacognitive processes for teachers to reflect on their practices. It provides well-defined guidance through the exploration of twelve constructs in the specific areas of questioning, self-assessment and feedback, observing and listening, explicit instruction, modeling and exemplars, support and safety, the use of time, setting expectations, connecting to student lifeworlds, desire to learn, resources, and existing knowledge. Further, it details what occurs when the most effective practices are evident but just as importantly what occurs when they are absent. *Teachers as Architects of Learning* goes a long way in addressing the challenge identified by Dinham and his colleagues (2008) of making best practice, common practice.

Janelle Wills

Chapter 1
Introduction

> I have come to realize that [as educators] our job is no different than those tasks carried out by architects and builders. We design, plan and orchestrate learning like an architect designs, plans and orchestrates buildings or structures. We then put on the builder's hard hat and try our best to construct the learning in a way our students will understand. While architects design and, in collaboration with builders, construct buildings, we construct the learning experience.
>
> —Peter McKinnon, curriculum leader and educator for twenty-nine years

One thing that became clear for us from very early on in our teaching careers was that one approach to teaching and learning does not support the learning of all students. As our careers evolved, we learned from our own successes and failures, through talking to and watching other teachers and consistently talking with our students in a way that showed them we wanted to help them with their work: learning. We began to wonder whether there was a correlation between how we were learning as teachers and the conditions we were putting in place for our students.

We struggled with questions such as the following: Why is it that some students seem to succeed and others don't? What do we say or do that works with students? What does not? Why is one strategy helpful for one student but not another? Why do we feel that we have to move ahead in our teaching when clearly our students haven't understood the initial concepts, key knowledge, and skills? What is it that we are doing that leads to success and failure with our students' learning? Why is there such disparity in teacher practice? What do we do with what we learn from watching others teach? Which way is the best way? In essence, we were making decisions about what was right for our students every day with a limited understanding of what we needed to consider from a learner's perspective.

Our subsequent work with teachers—as part of school leadership teams, as coaches, consultants, and mentors—indicated to us that many teachers are teaching without any due consideration to the process of learning, just as we had! Many teachers we have worked with express confusion, anxiety, and a sense of inadequacy in their teaching practice. The combination of a rapidly expanding research base for teaching and learning; pressure from government, society, community, parents, and colleagues to improve learning outcomes; and the very natural cognitive complexity of the teaching and the learning process can make teaching an exciting yet daunting profession. As our expectations for higher results increase, so does the need to understand some key constructs that build successful learning experiences.

We started to develop our theories on learning based on our own experiences as both students and teachers. It became clear that we needed to make a subtle change in our thinking—from *teaching and learning* to *learning and teaching*. The goal of the framework we present in this book is to increase levels of learning in classrooms through building understanding of learning, talking about learning, and reflecting on learning in a way that benefits the learner.

We make the distinction between *learning* and *teaching*, as often they are used in the same context. For teachers to become architects of learning, they need to consider those aspects of learning that enable students to develop their generative knowledge, which allows for retention, understanding, and active use of knowledge. Once teachers have identified and deeply understand critical constructs of learning, they can begin to see the implications in their planning and teaching. If teachers can't make those links, they will perceive any system or school initiative to improve teaching as an add-on and just something more to process in an already cloudy and clogged-up mind.

Focusing on the Learning

As teachers, we hear and read about student-centered learning often, yet the reality in the classroom, in our experience, can be very different. *Student-centered learning* refers to teaching practices that shift the emphasis in instructional decision-making processes from centering on teacher criteria to centering on learning impact. As part of an action research project with the Australian National Schools Network Curriculum Design Hub in Victoria, Australia, we asked teachers from twenty-two different elementary and high schools the following questions in relation to their curriculum planning.

- What's working well? (These are things you are proud of, that are going well, and that can be built on.)
- What's nonnegotiable? (These are things you don't like, that get in the way, or that you can't do much about.)
- What's a must-change? (These are the things you don't like but that can and must change.)

We collated the responses into those with a whole-school perspective, teacher perspective, or learner perspective; only a very small number of all responses mentioned the learner. Of those responses that mentioned the learner, there was some mention of learners but not learning; there were general comments about student engagement and individual student needs. We realized that although these responses were from educators in Australia, they could be applied anywhere in the world.

The core business for every school, teacher, and student is learning, so it struck us that we spend very little time at schools actually talking about the learning. There is little point in considering the teaching without understanding learning and what impacts it.

In fact, when we think about our own classroom teaching and our time spent in curriculum leadership roles, we realize we devoted most of our time to planning, teaching, and subsequent activities—but not to the learning.

Planning is teacher-focused should be learner-focused.

Learning needs to take more of a center stage in our schools and classrooms. Early on in our own classrooms, we often equated success with students who were on task, had completed what we had asked of them, or at least worked through it to the best of their ability, and had displayed a level of compliance to our expectations. While part of this was due to our limited time in the teaching profession, part of it was also influenced by school culture. The following are some (not all) of the cultural elements that were typical of our classroom-based experiences.

- We matched content to activities.
- We organized content week by week, often over the course of a semester.
- We got through all the standards or learning outcomes over a week, semester, and year.
- We viewed busy and compliant students as fully engaged.
- We felt that we didn't have the time to support all students because we had to move on to get through the content (after all, reports were due soon).
- We would often talk to the students about what was covered rather than what was learned.
- We incorporated many different programs and activities, making learning connections difficult to establish.
- We felt as though we had too much to do and not enough time to do it, and meetings about planning, reflection, and preparation kept us from our classrooms.
- We had many external interruptions to our program, making it impossible to do anything in depth.

Tchrs to judged on lesson plans & progression of the same.

These realities of school life contribute to a teacher's ongoing challenge, where the focus is entirely on teaching the content and not on learners learning the content.

John Hattie (2009) outlines key questions to ask so that educators can move away from the experiences we encountered by challenging traditional beliefs and conceptions about teaching and learning.

- How can we determine what is best to teach next without attending closely to what students already know?
- How can we choose materials without any evidence that these are the optimal materials?
- Why do we seek to keep students engaged and busy but not to ensure that they actually learn?
- Why do we choose activities that provoke the most interest, rather than asking what leads to students putting in effort? (Is it the effort, not the interest level of the activity, that is important?)
- How do we maximize the challenge of the learning goals and create structures for students to learn via the challenge, rather than structuring the material so that it is easy for students to learn?

I see this happening — easy lessons. But easy wins? or they at gr. level? or they?

What is focused on within a school environment reflects what is valued. Leaders must focus on learning and structure schools to allow teachers to do the same.

- Professional discussions should focus on student learning rather than on school organization and administration.
- Curriculum development should be based on what students need to know and how they are going to learn rather than on what needs to be covered. The majority of curriculum conversations should start with "What do our students need to know, and how can we plan to facilitate, teach, and support their learning?" rather than "What material do we need to cover?"
- Meeting schedules should be predominantly structured to suit the learning needs of students, not administrative needs that then take precious time away from our core purpose and away from time for teachers to collaborate around student learning.
- Teachers should have sufficient time to discuss, reflect on, and plan for their students' learning, rather than feeling overwhelmed with their additional responsibilities and frustrated that they do not have time.
- System initiatives should support and enhance teachers in their work, not redirect school focus.

It is not surprising that learning often does not take center stage. Quite often, survival is the focal point in classrooms, as educators and school leaders try to simply get through the week. Students have often expressed that they feel the same way. It is clear something has to drastically change.

The Key to Change: Some Promising Research

Research supports the need for change in mainstream education. Never before have we seen such a tide of optimism in being able to move from traditional schooling to schooling that truly centers on learning and supporting all students with greater urgency. The following lines of thinking could help improve the likelihood of success in learning for teachers, students, and ultimately the whole school.

- Schools need to develop a collective commitment to believing all students can and will learn at high levels (DuFour et al., 2016).
- Educators must understand fundamental constructs for learning to take learning to deeper, more meaningful levels for students.
- These constructs for learning have an impact on the instructional strategies that teachers develop and the way that they design the learning experience.
- The things we say and do as educators have an impact on learners; we must have a heightened awareness of this fact.
- We should be teaching for understanding. — *not new, Silver/Strong have said this for years*
- We should be creating learning spaces that respect and honor all students.

In our work with students, teachers, and leadership teams, we have sought to bring key pieces of research together to raise student achievement as we have grappled with the issues surrounding curriculum planning, effective teaching, and student learning to promote higher levels of student engagement.

Professional Learning Communities

One of the most substantial reforms in education is the transformation of schools into professional learning communities (PLCs). The work of Richard DuFour and colleagues (2016) has been highly influential in assisting schools to move from a culture centered on teaching to one centered on learning. Members of PLCs work in collaborative teams that focus on four critical questions.

1. What do we want each student to learn?
2. How will we know when each student has learned it?
3. How will we respond when a student experiences difficulty in learning?
4. How will we respond when a student already knows it?

The power of the PLC at Work® process is that it centers on results of learning before anything else. When we focus on learning, we give a clear message that this is what we value above all. Building a culture of professional learning that centers on learning, therefore, becomes pivotal to the chances of increasing student achievement in schools and to the building of the teacher as an architect of learning.

Teaching for Understanding

In the teaching-for-understanding framework, Perkins and Blythe (1994) describe four questions that teachers need to consider when planning for student learning where understanding is the goal.

1. What shall we teach?
2. What is worth understanding?
3. How shall we teach for understanding?
4. How can teachers and students understand, and how can students develop deeper understandings?

Perkins (1998) describes understanding as:

not just repeat whats just been done

> The ability to think and act flexibly with what one knows. . . . An understanding of a topic is a "flexible performance capability" with emphasis on the flexible. In keeping with this, learning for understanding is like learning a flexible performance—more like learning to improvise jazz or hold a good conversation or rock climb than learning the multiplication table or the dates of the presidents or F = MA. Learning facts can be a crucial backdrop to learning for understanding, but learning facts is not learning for understanding. (p. 40)

The work of Project Zero and its research around teaching for understanding has been instrumental in shaping our work with teachers. It has been refreshingly useful because it provides a voice in thinking through what we want or need learners to understand and then in building constructs around those understandings to make that happen.

The New Art and Science of Teaching

In *The New Art and Science of Teaching*, Robert Marzano (2017) outlines evidence that a great teacher can make a measurable difference to student learning. He also outlines forty-three instructional elements that have been shown to have a research-based higher probability for impact on learning when used in interrelated and specific ways. As he puts it:

> The more skill the artist exhibits with available techniques, the better his or her creations. Likewise, the more skill the classroom teacher has with the instructional strategies that research and theory have uncovered over the decades, the better the teacher will be able to create lessons that optimise student learning. (p. 2)

Marzano's instructional-design questions support teachers developing strategies to create the right learning conditions. Importantly, they ensure the criteria for success we are using lie in the impact our use of these strategies has on the learner.

Formative Assessment

The use of formative assessment (assessment *for* learning) is pivotal to becoming architects of learning. There are many definitions of *formative assessment*, but the one that correlates best with our work is Dylan Wiliam's (2018). He states:

> An assessment functions formatively to the extent that evidence about student achievement is elicited, interpreted, and used by teachers, learners, or their peers to make decisions about the next steps in instruction that are likely to be better, or better founded, than the decisions they would have made in the absence of that evidence. (p. 48)

In the United Kingdom, the Assessment Reform Group (1999) identifies that to improve learning through assessment, five key factors are required.

1. The provision of effective feedback to students
2. The active involvement of pupils in their own learning
3. Adjusting teaching to take account of the results of the assessment *The Tchr's job in formative Ass.*
4. A recognition of the profound influence assessment has on the motivation and self-esteem of pupils, both of which are crucial influences of learning
5. The need for pupils to be able to assess themselves and understand how to improve

Wiliam (2018) outlines five key strategies to support adapting teaching practice based on the needs of the learner.

Hattie, Fisher & Frey

1. Clarifying, sharing, and understanding learning intentions and criteria for success
2. Engineering effective classroom discussions, activities, and learning tasks that elicit evidence of learning
3. Providing feedback that moves learning forward
4. Activating learners as instructional resources for one another
5. Activating learners as the owners of their own learning

This focus on formative assessment highlights what successful teachers have been doing for a very long time. They choose tasks and teaching approaches to accurately ascertain where their students are, using this information to inform how they teach, while regularly monitoring learning growth as it evolves and subsequently adapting their approach to teaching. In essence, this work centers on how educators support students in their learning through being aware of the actions they take.

Productive Habits of the Mind

Finally, the work of Marzano (2006) again provides insight about how to build metacognitive capacities in our students. The importance of building these capacities in our students is significant. It prepares their minds to optimize their learning experiences.

Marzano (2006) divides productive *habits of mind* (Costa & Kallick, 2000a, 2000b) into three subcategories.

1. Self-regulated thinking and learning habits
2. Critical thinking and learning habits
3. Creative thinking and learning habits

By providing a learning culture that focuses on self-regulation and critical and creative thinking, both for students and for educators, the result is the development of enduring, lifelong, and able learners.

These key pieces of research greatly influence the constructs we outline in the framework in this book. Perkins and Blythe's (1994) work provides clues to how we can shape the learning experience so that learning is central. This is critical in the planning stage. Marzano (2017) helps us to consider instructional strategies for teachers that strengthen our chances of learning success. This fits into the teaching stage. Wiliam's (2018) work with formative assessment helps us to consider how we assist the learner to learn during the learning experience. The PLC process from DuFour et al. (2016) provides us with essential constructs for developing a collaborative and mindful culture for learning by providing a structure and capacity, for teachers and students alike, to inquire collaboratively into their own learning and practice.

For students to learn successfully, educators need to make a consistent and conscious attempt to address the following questions.

1. What is the correlation between what we have planned, how we have taught it, and what students have learned?
2. How are we preparing our students and ourselves for learning?
3. What might we learn from one another about this?

Teachers as Architects of Learning provides support for educators who are investigating these questions and endeavoring to put learning first.

Connections to Learning Theory

In addition to reflecting this important research, we have identified twelve learning constructs that include some of the key approaches and strategies from influential learning theory. Before examining the learning constructs, it is worth examining some of the learning theories that have shaped the way that we see education today. We took our responses from the action learning we conducted with teachers and correlated them with the most prominent learning theories that have shaped education over time, such as cognitivist, behaviorist, objectivist, constructivist, and social learning views. Table 1.1 (pp. 10–11) describes these prominent theories of learning and their subsequent implications for learning.

As these theories illustrate, learning isn't boxed or linear. Articulating how we learn is complex and is influenced by how we have learned, what we have read, and what has worked for us. A model of instruction or a theory on learning is just that: a model or a theory. As educators, we know that learning ebbs and flows, changing depending on environmental, political, cultural, and philosophical contexts. Even within the learning theories in table 1.1, each category may have derivative theories. For example, constructivism can be broken up into social constructivism and cognitive constructivism, bringing in elements of each of those views.

As architects of learning, teachers extrapolate on some of the key concepts from learning theories and infuse them into their practice mindfully. These include:

- Open-ended questioning (cognitivist)
- Metacognition (constructivist)
- Trial and error (constructivist)
- Reinforcement (behaviorist)
- Peer teaching (social learning)
- Modeling (all learning theories)
- Summative assessment (objectivist)
- Formative assessment (constructivist)
- Self-reflection (social learning and cognitivist)
- Direct instruction (behaviorist)
- Sequencing (objectivist)
- Building simplicity to complexity (constructivist)
- Clear objectives (objectivist, behaviorist)
- Rewards (behaviorist)
- Cooperative learning (social learning and constructivist)
- Graphic organizers (constructivist)
- Gradual release of responsibility (behaviorist) contd. on pg 12.

Table 1.1: Prominent Learning Theories Explained

	Cognitivist	**Behaviorist**	**Objectivist**	**Constructivist**	**Social Learning**
View of the Learner	Knowledge is developed through cognitive (thinking) processes that influence the way things are learned.	Knowledge is developed through conditioning students to behave in ways that compliment learning. The observed behavior is the focus.	Knowledge is external and is transferred from teachers to students.	Understanding and knowledge of the world is constructed through experiencing things and reflecting on those experiences.	Knowledge is learned through interacting and observing others. This theory has some links to observational learning.
Role of Teacher and View of Classroom	Students can't be forced to learn, so a teacher's role is to develop environments where thinking can be supported. Students actively make sense of the world through reconciling their existing perceptions with challenging tasks. They have an intrinsic motivation to want to know, and extrinsic motivation can undermine this. Students are provided thinking tools, asked lots of open-ended questions, and encouraged to learn from mistakes in order to reconceptualize their thinking.	Students learn through classical and operant conditioning. In essence, they are trained through the use of strategies such as associating positive events with learning, risk taking, breaking learning into smaller steps, noting similarities and differences, reinforcement of positive effort and behavior, explicit feedback for reinforcement, publicly recognizing established behaviors, and using cues as reminders.	Students learn by what they hear and through reading key material. A teacher assists by explaining key concepts clearly until the student understands it.	Learners construct their own knowledge by searching for meaning, interpreting what they hear, read, and see based on their previous knowledge and learning habits. Learners ask questions, explore, and assess what they know. A constructivist view to learning is supportive of David A. Kolb's (1984) model of experiential learning and Jerome Bruner's work around discovery learning.	Learners construct their own knowledge from paying attention to others and noticing what they do, retaining those behaviors through practice, feedback, coaching, and reinforcement. Learners can make decisions based on reward or punishments associated with particular behaviors. Human identity is central to learning in this way, as we develop our sense of self-identity and group identity through the way in which we interact with one another.

	Cognitivist	Behaviorist	Objectivist	Constructivist	Social Learning
Success Indicators	Learning is deemed successful when students are able to hypothesize, transfer knowledge into other areas, and articulate meaning to support memorization.	Learning is deemed successful when students can acquire knowledge and behave in ways that show a relationship with learning objectives explicitly made clear from the outset.	Learning is deemed successful when students can reiterate what has been taught. They are able to regurgitate the key pieces of knowledge in ways that make sense to the teacher.	Learning is successful when students can demonstrate and articulate conceptual understanding. They can reflect on what they have learned and identify where they need to take their learning now.	Learning is successful when students reproduce the initial behavior. They are able to make decisions about their learning based on what they have seen from others. They form their learning identity through taking cues from others and learning about themselves through their interactions.
Leading Theorists and Researchers	Piaget, Perkins, Gestalt, de Bono, Bloom, Glasser, Gagné	Skinner, Pavlov, Hunter, Popham, Ferster	Dick, Carey, Briggs, Wagner, Gagné	Bruner, Ausubel, Vygotsky, Ernest, Dewey, Piaget, Varela, von Glasersfeld	Ormrod, Bandura, Mayer, Sulzer-Azaroff, Rotter, Miller, Dollard, Rogers

- Student negotiation (social learning and cognitivist)
- Clear instructions (objectivist)
- Duplication and replication (behaviorist)
- Exemplars (social learning and cognitivist)
- Practice and review (objectivist)
- Memorizing (behaviorist)
- Making meaning (constructivist)
- Higher-order thinking (cognitivist)
- Concept-based learning (cognitivist)
- Real-life application (constructivist)
- Generating attention and interest (behaviorist)
- Goal setting (constructivist)
- Prior knowledge (behaviorist and constructivist)
- Competency levels (objectivist)
- Demonstrating collaboration (social learning)
- Exploration (cognitivist and constructivist)
- Deeper thinking (cognitivist)

When we list key approaches and strategies, in order to better make sense of them, there may be a danger that we see them as disconnected from one another. However, when summarizing some of the key approaches and strategies that represent each theory on learning, it is important to note that they are interconnected. The purpose of sharing these approaches and strategies is to support their synthesis into constructs for learning that teachers can use to make more informed decisions in relation to their practice. This forms the basis of our ideas in this book.

We propose that the important work to be done in education is this: to reconcile what we understand about learning from being a learner with what we can learn about learning from key research, then challenge ourselves to ensure that our approaches successfully work for our students through the ongoing and mindful refinement of our teaching practice.

The Building of Teaching Wisdom

This book is intended to assist teachers or anyone in the position of leading learning to build their wisdom around the art of teaching in order for deeper learning to prevail. It aims to support teachers to deconstruct their mental models in order to then construct new learning about their practice. These insights assist them in identifying beliefs that impact their behaviors as their teaching architecture evolves. The premise that beliefs influence behaviors is at the heart of *Teacher as Architects of Learning*.

As teachers develop insight into their beliefs and practice, they are developing their wisdom. We use the term *wisdom* to mean "having insight into ourselves and knowing what to do with it." A teacher who is developing wisdom around his or her practice can act on that wisdom in ways to allow learning to prevail.

For example, teachers who consciously and deliberately develop their wisdom are more metacognitive in their approach to teaching and learning. They model their practice so that others can learn from them and observe others in action, learning from them. They are clear about their beliefs and principles and can articulate both what they do and why they do it.

Teachers who are developing their wisdom make sound judgments in relation to planning, teaching, and learning from experience and knowledge. They are sagacious in that they can utilize this knowledge in a practical sense to support their students' learning. They are alert, crafty, and smart in their approach to their work and avoid rashness in decision making. They apply knowledge, understanding, experience, discretion, and intuitive understanding when meeting the challenges of activating learning.

This book supports teachers in the development of their wisdom. It draws from personal experiences and research, the research and ideas of others, and the reflections of teachers themselves to serve as a catalyst for thinking about their own practice in a way that lets learning lead.

This book is based on the premise that, for learning to succeed, we need to understand learning. It is designed to enable teachers to build their expertise, knowledge, skills, experiences, and successes or failures in a way that contributes to the building of their teaching wisdom and therefore the building of their professional practice.

We propose twelve constructs for learning for your consideration. They are at the core of the mission for teachers who want to become architects of learning through the process of building their teaching wisdom.

The *Teachers as Architects of Learning* Mission

To understand the mission of this work, it is important to understand the analogy of an architect. The role of an architect is often described as designing and configuring buildings. To design is to make decisions about how elements look, and to configure is to arrange those elements in a particular way. The role of a teacher as an architect of learning is to design and configure learning experiences. To design is to make decisions about how the learning experience will look. To configure is to arrange the learning experience in a particular way. These instructional decisions are the catalyst to successful learning and by extension the effectiveness of the teacher.

The development of a teacher's architecture therefore will involve ongoing processes of inquiry and discovery as teachers find out what works best for them and the learners they serve. They develop a personal architectural blueprint for teaching that has them consider the very strategies, techniques, and approaches required to successfully impact the learner. This architecture shifts and changes over time but is always based on the difference their approach to teaching makes.

Teachers as Architects of Learning supports teachers in achieving three fundamental goals.

1. To activate successful student learning
2. To grow in consciousness about how intentional teaching practices impact successful learning
3. To learn through reflection both on and in action (Schön, 1983)

To Activate Successful Student Learning

We achieve this goal through increasing the likelihood of meeting the needs of learners by closing the gap between what is planned, how it's taught, and what students actually learn as a result of the learning experience.

The *learning experience* is what learners actually experience as they are supported in their learning—the total sum of what they have done to come to learn something.

In order for a learning experience to be successful, it must result in the acquisition of *generative knowledge* as opposed to *fragile knowledge.* It is generative knowledge that we seek in the learner (Perkins & Blythe, 1994). Figure 1.1 (page 15) contrasts generative and fragile knowledge as explained by Grift and Satchwell (2007) and based on the work of David Perkins and Tina Blythe (1994).

Generative knowledge, which requires "good" thinking and focuses on:	Rather than	Fragile knowledge, which can be:
• Retention of knowledge • Understanding of knowledge • Active use of knowledge		• Missing (The student has been exposed to it but can't remember it.) • Inert (The knowledge is there, but the student can't do anything with it.) • Naive (The information is simplistic, stereotypical, or wrong.) • Ritualistic (The information is useful for a school task and nothing more.)

Figure 1.1: Generative versus fragile knowledge.

What makes generative knowledge preferred is that it:

- Transfers to other situations
- Makes a difference to the learner (so that it contributes to enhancing his or her life or the lives of others)
- Assists in developing curiosity within the learner
- Supports the individual learner in a personalized way

To Grow in Consciousness About How Intentional Teaching Practices Impact Successful Learning

Raising consciousness levels enables teachers to:

- Make more informed decisions about what they do every day in the classroom
- Lead a more successful learning experience for their students

Arthur L. Costa, Robert J. Garmston, and Diane P. Zimmerman (2014) define people who enjoy a state of consciousness as those who:

> Monitor their own values, intentions, thoughts, and behaviors and their effects on others and the environment. They have well-defined value systems that they can articulate. They generate, hold, and apply internal criteria for decisions they make. . . . They practice mental rehearsal and the editing of mental pictures in the process of seeking improved strategies. (p. 26)

This heightened level of consciousness and deliberate practice is an important shift to becoming more proficient as an architect of learning.

To Learn Through Reflection Both on and in Action

This goal provides an opportunity to reflect on our own teaching practice through a four-stage action learning approach of:

- Thinking
- Planning
- Acting
- Reflecting

Thomasina D. Piercy (as cited in Psencik, 2009) outlines the importance of this goal: "We learn from processing our experiences and we enlarge our frame of reference beyond the episodic" (p. 96). Carmen Friesen from the Tulare County Office of Education (as cited in Costa, Garmston, Ellison, & Hayes, 2016) encapsulates the importance of reflection when she states:

> I hear and I forget,
>
> I see and I remember,
>
> I do and I understand,
>
> I reflect and I learn.

This book is designed for teachers who are committed to deliberately improving their instruction through thinking, planning, acting, and reflecting in order to adapt their practice. They take stock of the effectiveness of their practice and identify where they want to move it toward: a deliberate process for developing constructs of thinking that supports a metacognitive approach to teaching and ensures commitment to ongoing, steadfast professional growth.

The Twelve Constructs Defined

We identified the twelve constructs for learning that we present in this book through our work with more than forty elementary and secondary schools. Through action-learning projects, we investigated the link between how humans learn and what teachers provide in their classrooms. We asked school leadership, teachers, and support staff from these schools three questions based on the Teaching for Understanding project work undertaken by the Project Zero team at the Harvard Graduate School of Education. We chose the questions to encourage teachers to consider learning from their own experiences. We operated from the assumption that we can all find examples of when we have been successful in our learning and we can recall the conditions required for us to be successful in that learning. We surmised that the responses to these questions could reveal the prevalent constructs required for deep learning to thrive.

Participants were asked to think of something that they have come to know deeply—something that they've come to know how to do successfully. Then we posed the following three questions.

1. What did you have to do to learn it?
2. How do you know you've learned it?
3. What evidence do you have that you have learned it?

We categorized the responses we received from the participants and used them to form twelve constructs for designing and configuring a successful learning experience. This was done through recording all the responses, categorizing them into areas of similarity, and then attaching a concept label to the elements that were consistently surfacing. For example, if someone learned how to ski and somebody else learned how to play the violin, both agreed that time to practice was critical. Relating this to classrooms, the use of time has important implications for students when teachers construct the learning experience.

Typical responses to the questions from participants included (but were not limited to):

1. What did you have to do to learn it?
   - See it in action
   - Read instructions
   - Have it explained
   - Practice it over
   - Receive feedback
   - Trial and error

2. How do you know you've learned it?
   - The feedback received
   - The improvement noticed over time
   - Can teach it to someone else
   - The time it takes to execute has reduced
   - Success in the task or application of the learning
   - Can apply it to other contexts

3. What evidence do you have that you have learned it?
   - Confident using it or doing it
   - Can answer questions about it
   - Innate feeling
   - Recognition from outside sources
   - Successful performance, application, or product

In this context, the term *construct* means the elements that need to be in place when we are learning something to give us the best chance of succeeding in the learning. They are the circumstances that have occurred throughout the learning experience enabling the learner to learn. As teachers, we try to create this set of circumstances within the learning experience to give our students the best chance of learning, rather than leaving learning to chance.

The Twelve Constructs for a Successful Learning Experience

The twelve constructs for learning outlined in this book are as follows.

1. Questioning

   Effectively used, questions create the platform for ensuring teachers and students understand where learners are in their understanding, they provide the catalyst for motivating students to further their learning efforts, and they contribute to a classroom culture that promotes curiosity, wonder, and reciprocal respect while safeguarding learning as the number-one priority. Effective questions are also paramount in informing teachers about what they might need to do next in their support of the learning process.

2. Self-assessment—reflection and feedback

   Student involvement in which students are able to clearly articulate and monitor their learning progression is critical in building the self-efficacy in students. Opportunity for significant self-assessment that encompasses structured, meaningful, and targeted reflection and feedback becomes a powerful tool for learners to monitor their efforts and plot their path for future learning success. The capacity for teachers to build self-assessment into their practice also provides teachers with the critical information they may need from students to clarify students' thinking, better address misconceptions or errors in reasoning, and find what assists their learning. This can only be done when we move the emphasis from feeding back to students toward receiving feedback from students.

3. Observing and listening

The role of sensory learning is ever present in the teacher–learner relationship. A teacher who is able to observe how a student is coping or empathize with a student's struggles may be able to more appropriately respond to the student's needs. When the teacher truly listens to what the student is saying, the student's thinking processes can be illuminated to truly provide a window into the mind. Moreover, when a teacher can create a climate where students recognize and apply the skills of deep listening and targeted observing, they too are a step closer to developing learning dispositions that place them in good stead both within and beyond the school.

4. Explicit instruction

The enemy of explicit instruction is ambiguity. Teachers who utilize the key elements to this behaviorist approach to teaching ensure the learning for students is clear, understood, practiced, reinforced, and guided. Teachers who use explicit instruction don't leave learning to chance and can apply it when used skillfully to a range of learning contexts. Even within an inquiry learning unit of work, students may need the skills for research specifically taught, for example. To teach instruction explicitly, teachers rely on their clear understanding of the intended understandings and the instructional processes required in order for students to demonstrate they have learned and can apply this learning.

5. Modeling and exemplars

It's a genuine challenge to work toward something you haven't seen, touched, or experienced. Demonstrating, discussing, and analyzing exemplar models of products or processes provides students with the mental model they need to apply successful approaches to the learning process. Providing students with this opportunity can remove "secret service" teaching, whereby students only know how successful they have been once they've been allocated their final grade or mark for a task or course.

6. Support and safety

Trust is foundational to learning, and a safe and supportive environment is the platform for building relational trust. Students who feel connected, physically and psychologically safe, and supported within their classroom environment will be more willing to take risks in both their academic and social and emotional learning. Within this construct lie the decisions teachers make about the physical environment they set up, the rules and procedures they implement, and the methodology they apply to the building of relationships in their classroom. The outcome of applying this construct well is a decreased sense of vulnerability in students and therefore higher levels of trust and possible engagement in the learning process.

7. Time

We do not get more time. We can only work with the time we have in our schools and classrooms. This construct considers deeply not the question around how much time we have but rather how we use our time effectively when we teach. This relies on decisions made through planning, prioritizing, and maintaining focus. It is critical because of the simple fact that once the time has passed, you can't go back to get it. Every minute matters in the learning process, and that's the first priority any teacher makes when considering this construct.

8. Expectations

You get what you expect, so what are you expecting? This construct is perceptual in that even when teachers believe they have high expectations for learning and communicate a belief in students' ability to succeed, the students themselves might not see it this way. This is why it is both challenging and essential. Expectancy is the belief that with further effort the learner will improve and succeed. Expectancy is affected by things such as the quality and level of support provided, available resources at hand, and the dispositions and skills of the learner.

9. Lifeworlds

Teachers and students bring to their learning experience each day the world in which they have come from and the form that it has taken in their dispositions. According to Hattie (2003), up to 60 percent of variance in student achievement can be attributed to what students bring to the learning experience themselves that is important. This construct assists teachers in recognizing this to be a factor and then creating a mindset to respect and connect to the lifeworlds of the students but to never allow it to diminish the expectations teachers have of what students can achieve.

10. Desire

Desire links to the motivation to learn. This construct asks teachers to consider how they honor what students bring to the learning in terms of their motivation to learn it. There are times when little external thought needs to be given because students are naturally curious and interested in what is taught. There are other times when it pays for teachers to think about the strategies and techniques they can bring to the learning experience to spark interest, curiosity, and a desire to find out more.

11. Resources

    This construct has teachers consider what are the most appropriate, effective, and powerful human and nonhuman resources that can foster learning success. It's less about having resources and more about basing instructional decisions on how and when to best use the resources we have. It requires a view that outside of the teachers and students themselves (who are both human resources to the learning) other resources might need to be utilized.

12. Existing knowledge

    This construct recognizes and builds from the knowledge and skills a learner already possesses. It encourages teachers to consider how they will access and utilize the prior knowledge students have to aid others in their learning and to ensure the instruction is pitched to their relevant stage of developmental readiness. Accessing prior knowledge is also critical in acting as a filter for teachers as they determine the need for differentiating content.

Thinking about our work in relation to these constructs enables us to examine, question, and explore our beliefs and their subsequent actions through the lens of learning with the view to finding opportunities for growth. This gives us a greater opportunity to challenge our perceptions of why we do what we do in order to make some genuine second-order changes to our practice because our thinking has changed in fundamental ways (Marzano, Waters, & McNulty, 2005).

Table 1.2 lists the twelve constructs along with how teachers use them to aid learning and how students learn when each construct is in place.

Table 1.2: The Twelve Constructs for a Successful Learning Experience

Constructs	Teachers Aid Learning by ...	Learners Learn by ...
Questioning	Asking purposeful questions of the learner	Generating and asking questions to clarify and make meaning
Self-assessment: reflection and feedback	Explicitly involving students at a metacognitive level in the learning experience	Understanding their own work at a deeper level and accurately self-assessing
Observing and listening	Observing students' input and output	Observing the thoughts and actions of both themselves and others
Explicit instruction	Providing instruction to learners	Having access to instructional support when needed

Constructs	Teachers Aid Learning by ...	Learners Learn by ...
Modeling and exemplars	Modeling behaviors, thinking, and exemplars for the learner	Having models and exemplars that support the learning
Support and safety	Providing a safe and supportive environment for the learner	Enabling and seeking support and feeling comfortable in doing so
Time	Structuring time in a flexible manner for the learner to develop and deepen his or her understanding	Using time effectively and having time to develop and deepen understanding
Expectations	Establishing and articulating expectations for the learner	Working toward expectations that are challenging and achievable
Lifeworlds	Connecting to the lifeworld of the learner	Connecting the learning to their own lifeworlds
Desire	Generating a desire for learning	Seeing a relevance, or having an interest in or a need for the learning—and therefore a desire to learn it
Resources	Providing human and nonhuman resources for learners	Using resources to support learning
Existing knowledge	Capitalizing on the existing knowledge of the learner	Drawing from existing knowledge

By using these twelve constructs, it is our intention that teachers will behave differently during the teaching of planning of learning experiences and thus see better results as an outcome of their hard work. Teachers use the constructs to consciously reflect on their teaching of a unit, course, or lesson. This helps them become more successful in supporting the learning of their students. The constructs are a practical way of ensuring that learning is central to the decisions teachers make about teaching every day; teachers ensure that the choices they make are based on learners' needs rather than on their own interests, preferences, habits, needs, and plans. The twelve constructs keep the learner, rather than the activity or process, at the heart of the teaching. The twelve constructs include strategies that support diverse learners—it's not a one-size-fits-all approach. Teachers have the autonomy to make decisions for using an explicit teaching approach within the negotiated curriculum to illustrate this point. The approach is compatible with outcomes, such as the achievement standards outlined in the Common Core State Standards Initiative, that require learners meet certain targets (National Governors Association Center for Best Practices & Council of Chief State School Officers, 2010). For example, if the standard in fourth-grade social studies expects students to construct historical narratives using key ideas and images from graphic and written sources when inquiring into the past, then a teacher may decide considering the construct for:

- The use of *time* when allocating lessons across the learning cycle
- *Explicit instruction* of key inquiry skills required to successfully do this
- *Existing knowledge* form their work on narratives in English
- *Desire* to find strategies that hook students into the concepts associated with this aspect of history

The twelve constructs combine the needs of the learner with the key concepts, knowledge, and skills they are required to learn.

Importantly, teachers can use the twelve constructs in an eclectic sense and regardless of the curriculum they are working with or the educational theories from which their beliefs might be formed. The range of constructs a teacher chooses to design and configure the learning experience will vary depending on the context. For example, when working with students who are struggling in their capacity to read for understanding, a teacher may choose to utilize strategies more akin to *explicit instruction* than a teacher who is working with a highly able reader. This teacher may draw more from the construct of *questioning* to support and deepen the student's understanding of a particular text.

With all the complexities of working as a teacher, it is easy to lose sight of the core business of education: learning. Examining one's teaching and design for learning with the twelve constructs in mind provides teachers with the opportunity to stop being distracted by those things that are not conducive to student learning. This way, educators can begin to disregard things that get in the way and focus collaboratively on learning and the results that flow from it.

How to Use This Book

Teachers as Architects of Learning will support you in developing ideas, considering approaches, and, in general, increasing your level of consciousness about what you do, why you do it, and how you might do it differently. The goal is to support you in enhancing your professional practice to ensure learning success for all your students.

This book will be helpful for anyone who has the responsibility of planning and implementing a learning experience. This includes those from mainstream education and those outside of it. We have written the book so that it is accessible to a variety of practitioners regardless of their context. This may include, but is not limited to, the following.

- Early childhood teachers
- Elementary school teachers
- Secondary school teachers
- Undergraduate teachers
- Tertiary educators
- Learning support specialists
- Specialist subject teachers
- Special education teachers
- Private tutors
- Program planners
- School principals
- Educational coaches
- Program writers and developers
- Casual relief teachers
- Community education teachers and trainers
- Vocational leaders and teachers
- Curriculum writers
- Collaborative teams of educators
- Corporate training and development leaders or trainers
- Anyone passionate about learning

We have made every effort to ensure that readers have the opportunity to reflect on their own context and practices to give their learning experiences the greatest chance of success.

There are many ways educators can use this book to support their planning and implementing of a successful learning experience. Again, ways may include, but are not limited to:

- Teams of teachers inquiring into ways of improving their practice to increase the likelihood of reaching high levels of learning for all students
- Individual teachers looking for different ways to approach their teaching practice in order to be the best teachers they can be
- Curriculum writers and program developers committed to ensuring they consider the learning experience rather than just the content when designing a program for the learner
- Consultants or coaches as they assist educators they may be working with to improve their effectiveness as teachers
- Educators looking for a reflective tool to encourage discussion and dialogue within their practice and profession

- School principals looking for a tool to promote an action-oriented approach centering on learning but designed to support the development of teaching practice
- Any leaders of learning who may be looking for strategies to improve what they do for the learners they serve

How This Book Is Structured

Each chapter of this book focuses on one of the twelve constructs of a successful learning environment. Chapters 2 to 13 investigate the constructs in depth. The structure of each chapter is the same. We begin by providing the reader with a working definition to provide clarity and then promote practical application through the following structure.

- **Rationale:** Highlights the reasons behind the importance of the construct.
- **Strategies to consider:** Provides the reader with actual strategies to put the construct into action.
    - **Putting the learning into context: sample scenarios**—This section offers an understanding of what the construct looks like, sounds like, and feels like in the reality of a teaching and learning experience.
    - **When the construct is missing and when it is evident**—These sections show the symptoms and evidence of a learning environment in which the construct is in use and when it is not.
    - **Think and reflect**—This section supports our mission to facilitate growth of the mindful teacher. It includes questions for reflection for individuals or those working in collaboration that will bring about an awareness of how the construct can become a sustained part of the reader's teaching practice.
- **Supporting ideas and research:** This section supports readers who want further information on the ideas within the chapter. We have included this section to help readers with their ongoing commitment to professional learning in their chosen area.

Conclusion

We began this chapter with words from an educator—Peter McKinnon—who spoke of the similarities between educators and architects and builders. In the same email to us, Peter continued his reflection with the following words that expressed his frustration with feeling disengaged with his profession as the years have passed:

However, I lost my designs, plans, and hard hat years ago. As my teaching career has progressed, I have felt more submissive with every new initiative. New information has made things more complex, and I have no time to process it. The subservience I feel has disengaged me from the profession. I feel less like an architect and more like a robot. This feeling resonates through my students, I'm sure.

We conclude this chapter with the rest of Peter's comments, which he shared at the conclusion of a five-day *Teachers as Architects of Learning* institute, where he had the opportunity to learn about the twelve constructs of a successful learning experience:

What we did over the five days together has provided me with an opportunity to reassess. I now have models, processes, and tools that will enable my students to learn deeply. I have reflected on how what I currently do impacts how and what my students learn. Most importantly, I have reconnected to:

- *What it means to learn*
- *What that means for my students*
- *What that means for me*
- *What it means to work collaboratively*
- *The implications all this has on my planning*

Peter McKinnon, curriculum leader and educator for twenty-nine years
(personal communication, November 2013)

In this introductory chapter, we have outlined some promising research that supports the shift in education from a focus on the teaching to a focus on the learning. We described the learning theories that have historically influenced the actions teachers have adopted in their practice and the implications of this on the learning experience. We proposed that teachers as architects of learning would be wise to consider the constructs associated with both learning theory and personal experience to inform their instructional decisions to put learning first.

The following chapter will outline, in depth, the construct for questioning when designing and configuring a successful learning experience.

Chapter 2
Questioning

> Any knowledge that doesn't lead to new questions quickly dies out: it fails to maintain the temperature required for sustaining life.
>
> —Wislawa Szymborska

Questions are invitational statements aimed at gaining information, exploring ideas and opinions, crystallizing thoughts, and extending thinking. The art of questioning provides learners and teachers with opportunities for deep exploration and clarification through thoughtful provocations.

Rationale

Questioning is central to the job of both learner and teacher. On any given day, teachers spend a lot of time asking questions of learners. Questioning is viewed by leaders in the field as essential to the building of a successful learning experience. Marzano (2017) outlines the critical importance of questioning through considering strategies for teachers to have students review content, elaborate on information, increase response rates, and engage reluctant learners.

It is important to understand the intention behind a question when exploring this construct. What is the purpose of a question? What thinking is being sought? In what ways might the question support new learning? In what ways can a question contribute to a greater depth of understanding? Reasons for asking questions include:

- To interest and engage learners
- To challenge existing attitudes, perceptions, and beliefs
- To stimulate recall for existing knowledge in a way that leads learners to reconcile new ideas and concepts
- To narrow the learners' thinking to the key concepts, knowledge, and skills being taught
- To revise key understandings and support the sequential construction of knowledge

- To promote thinking to the point where learners can make hypotheses
- To support the building of metacognition
- To help the learner move to deeper levels of thinking, such as with models of questioning built around Benjamin Bloom's taxonomy of knowledge, comprehension, application, analysis, synthesis, and evaluation (Bloom, Engelhart, Furst, Hill, & Krathwohl, 1956)—for example:
  - When was gold first discovered in California?
  - What do you think happened as a result of the discovery?
  - From these events, can you create a timeline showing when they occurred?
  - How would our society look today if gold hadn't been discovered?
  - How do these events compare to what we know about?
  - What might be the pros and cons of the discovery of gold?

For teachers to become architects of learning, they must have the goal of developing generative knowledge over fragile knowledge, therefore increasing the levels of questioning. Teachers must ask lower cognitive questions (recall, fact, closed, direct, and knowledge based) and higher cognitive questions (open ended, inquiry, inferential, and interpretive) in ways that foster deeper understandings. To ask the right questions at the right level, we must first be clear about what thinking we need from the learner and what our expectations are for each learning experience. Then we can be more deliberate in the types of questions we ask.

Questioning Strategies to Consider

In practice, asking questions that aid the learner can be complex work. The following three questioning strategies can assist you in planning and asking the right questions.

1. **Have a clear purpose:** Understand the reason you are asking the question and your intended outcome. If we aren't clear and deliberate in the questions we ask of the learner, we may be making the learning more complex and unattainable than it has to be. For example, when a teacher is wanting to find out how much a student understands about the power of marketing in persuading people, this is a good question: When you think about elements in the advertisement that might be deliberately trying to sway you to think a certain way, what might some of those elements be? This is a less effective question: So what is this advertisement telling you?

   The first question demonstrates the teacher knows what he or she wants the student to understand and communicates to the student what is important. The second question is too broad and for this context doesn't relate specifically to the outcome being sought.

2. **Promote a safe and supportive questioning environment:** Ensure that learners feel confident in asking and answering questions. If learners are inhibited from asking and answering questions that connect to what they may be processing, reconciling, or reflecting on, they lose a tremendous opportunity to be successful in their learning. Questions play a critical role in the development of relationships with learners. It is one of the most powerful tools teachers have to find out about the world of the student they are teaching. One way of building respectful relationships is to question students on their attitudes, beliefs, experiences, and thoughts in a manner that enables you to get to know them personally.

3. **Develop productive questioning practice:** Be mindful about how you are going to ask questions—not only what you ask but how you ask it. This will impact greatly on the individual learning experience. Focusing on both the content and the delivery of questions may bring us closer to bridging the gap between successful teaching and learning. The way you ask questions can go a long way to building trust between teacher and learner. For example, think about your tone and intonation as you ask questions.

   - Are you approachable or interrogational?
   - Are you interested or dismissive?
   - Are you unpretentious or patronizing?
   - Are you friendly or aloof?
   - Are you positive or negative?
   - Are you affectionate or detached?
   - Are you calm or ruffled?
   - Are you empathetic or insensitive?

   Putting this into the classroom context, consider a teacher who asks a student, "Why did you decide to put the comma there?" Depending on the tone and intonation used by the teacher, the student could perceive that either he or she has done the wrong thing or the teacher genuinely is interested in his or her thought process. Here is another question to consider: What on earth were you thinking? Depending on the tone and intonation, again, this could be construed as either very patronizing (therefore insensitive) or caring (therefore empathetic).

Table 2.1 (page 30) lists additional questioning dos and don'ts from the research of Paul Black and Dylan Wiliam (2004) on the impact of formative assessment on student learning. We have linked these to our three key strategies by indicating in parentheses which strategy the dos most closely correlate with (purpose, practice, or environment).

Table 2.1: Questioning Dos and Don'ts

Questioning Dos	Questioning Don'ts
Do plan carefully crafted questions that support your intention (purpose).	Don't be unclear about why you are asking the questions.
Do just tell students (not question) when you want them to know something (practice).	Don't use too many closed questions that could simply be stated as instructions.
Do partner students to process higher cognitive questions together (environment).	Don't jump too quickly into higher cognitive questions.
Do plan your questions (purpose and practice).	Don't ask questions that are superficial or so many questions that they lead to confusion.
Do give students at least three seconds of waiting time; we all need processing time when we have been given a question (practice).	Don't answer the questions that you have posed yourself.
Do acknowledge all answers respectfully. If you want a particular answer, consider just telling your students (environment).	Don't ask open-ended questions when you have the actual answer in mind; don't play the guess-what's-in-my-head game.
Do include no-hands-up sessions where students respond to questions from the teacher by being asked directly rather than by putting their hands up to enable students to be more accountable. Have students record or talk to one another about the question before reporting back (environment).	Don't ask the same few students the majority of your questions.
Do encourage students to respond to one another's answers respectfully. Show empathy in your responses to students: "I understand why you would think that …" (environment and practice).	Don't address misconceptions or mistakes ineffectively, such as "No, you are way off beam with that response" or "No, that's wrong." It's not that it's *bad* practice to identify something as wrong; it's just more effective when you outline reasons why and recognize students' thinking.
Do ask students to explain more about their thinking, and recognize when students are thinking—even when they are wrong (purpose, practice, and environment).	Don't treat student responses inequitably and inappropriately, such as "Yes, OK, but I like Peter's response better" or "You are not thinking straight."

Source: Adapted from Black & Wiliam, 2004.

Putting the Learning in Context: Sample Scenarios

Consider the following scenario where we outline the same learning experience in two different ways: one that is inclusive of the construct for questioning and one that is not.

Peter Mooney is providing a lesson on brain-based learning strategies to assist independent study habits for his tenth-grade students in preparation for their exams.

Scenario One

The students assemble in his class and take their seats. Students take out their notebooks or laptops. Peter begins his presentation outlining the key concepts he is going to cover throughout the sixty minutes. He then proceeds to talk though his slides for thirty minutes, asking some rhetorical questions (because they don't require an answer and he doesn't wait for one) along the way, such as "What's the matter with students' study habits today?" and "How much longer do I need to be making this point?" Peter doesn't pause to reflect either for himself or for the students. At the halfway point, he stops and asks the students to note any connections they might be making with the content and experiences they have had in their study habits: "What connection are you making to your experience when studying?" He gives the students two minutes to do so. For the remainder of the lecture, he continues to discuss the content of his slides. In the last minute, he suggests the students think about a quote he has on the screen, as they will be discussing it at the beginning of their next class. He concludes the lesson with two minutes to spare with "Who has any questions?"

Scenario Two

The students assemble in the classroom and take their seats. Students take out their notebooks or laptops. Peter looks out at them and asks the students to respond to the following prompt he has put up on the screen: "Students don't need a planned approach to study. What they need are clear strategies to help them and natural consequences for the effort they make. Why might you agree or disagree with this statement? Turn and talk to your neighbor."

After five minutes, Peter draws them back in and shares some research on the benefits of productive independent study habits and defines what he means by the term *productive*. He then spends ten minutes sharing some key concepts and supporting research. He again stops and asks the students to respond to a question that relates to their personal experience as students at the elementary and secondary levels: "How does this compare with how you have approached your study in the past?" He continues to chunk his lesson like this, stopping approximately every ten minutes and asking the students to respond to a question he has deliberately framed around the specific content. In the last ten minutes of the lecture, he pauses and asks students to individually or collectively write down questions they now have. He explains that they will be expected to ask these within the first part of the next class period. He finishes with the same quote as in the first scenario.

In the second example, Peter has carefully and deliberately crafted his questions to support his students' understanding:

- By posing a question that has them engage with the topic and preview what the key learning of the lesson will be about
- By stopping periodically and posing a relevant question that encourages them to make sense of the concepts both from a personal perspective and through the information he has shared
- By inviting students to craft their own questions that relate to their level of understanding, both demonstrating respect for their knowledge and forecasting the link to the next progression of learning

When Effective Questioning Is Missing

When effective questioning is missing, the learning environment may show some of the following symptoms.

- Students show a lack of interest and engagement in the content of the lesson. For example, students may spend an entire learning experience showing no evidence that they have processed anything by:
  - Taking and scrawling unrelated notes
  - Talking with their peers at inappropriate times
  - Spending the entire lesson saying nothing
  - Having difficulty coping with tasks and giving up
  - Finding it difficult to relate the content to previous learning
  - Displaying a behavior of indifference when asked to contribute
  - Displaying elements of passivity, such as:
    - Lack of eye contact
    - Looking around (daydreaming)
    - Looking down at books
    - Not writing, recording, or responding
    - Withdrawing mentally and physically from the environment

- Teachers may seem to spend the majority of the lesson talking at students or having them work on an activity with minimal interaction. Typically, a learning experience without high-level questioning will illuminate whether the teacher or the activity becomes the key focus of the learning experience—rather than the learning itself.

When Effective Questioning Is Evident

A learning culture where questioning is mindfully incorporated will show evidence of:

- Students connecting prior knowledge to current content in discussions.
- The teacher sharing prepared questions throughout a lesson. For example, a teacher asks a question and then records it on a whiteboard, screen, or piece of student work.
- Pauses that come after a teacher or student asks a question, after a teacher or student has responded to a question, and before the teacher or student asks the question.
- Sound assessment practices, as there may be a clear correlation between what a teacher finds out about his or her students' understanding and the crafting of a question to support them moving forward. For example, "Given what you have just discovered, what might you need to apply to your next piece of work to take it to the next level?"
- Teachers and students speaking with a tone that encourages others to think and respond.
- Dialogue that focuses as much on growth in learning and discovery as it does on the right answer.
- The use of purposeful questions designed to elicit specific responses, such as:
  - Knowledge retrieval
  - Individual reflections
  - Creative thinking and solutions
  - Links to other learning experiences
  - Engagement to the content
  - Connections between the learning and the real world of the student

Think and Reflect

1. What things have an impact on the way you and your students express and answer questions?
2. In what ways does questioning support the learning of your students?
3. What is your default way of questioning?
4. Would all your students perceive your questions as supportive?
5. What happens to your questions when you are tired, in a rush, and so forth? Do you do any of the following?
   - Spend less time thinking about the questions you ask
   - Ask fewer questions through reverting to telling
   - Change in intonation and expression
6. Is there a particular strategy you can identify that you need to develop further?
7. When you think about colleagues you know who seem to ask effective questions, what might they be doing that correlates with the information in this chapter?
8. How might this section on questioning support you in the development of your teaching practice?

Supporting Ideas and Research

The following resources provide additional information and ideas you can use to further develop your knowledge of questioning.

Bransford, J. D., Brown, A. L., & Cocking, R. R. (2000). *How people learn: Brain, mind, experience, and school* (Expanded ed.). Washington, DC: National Academies Press. The authors discuss the art of questioning throughout this book. As with many other texts, the focus is on giving students (not just teachers) the skills to become the questioner.

Fisher, D., & Frey, N. (2014). *Checking for understanding: Formative assessment techniques for your classroom* (2nd ed.) Alexandria, VA: Association for Supervision and Curriculum Development. Fisher and Frey outline the what and how of questioning to ensure teachers check for understanding and use questions for learning. The strategies and tips provided are very informative.

Hattie, J. A. C. (2009). *Visible learning*. London: Routledge. This book challenges the way teachers use questions and reports that not all questioning techniques are effective in improving student learning. The author emphasizes the importance of teaching students the skills of questioning.

International Baccalaureate Primary Years Programme—*www.ibo.org/pyp*. Focuses on the concept and the use of questioning to promote inquiry.

James Nottingham—*www.jamesnottingham.co.uk*. Nottingham (researcher and author) explores some interesting questioning techniques to challenge students' thinking.

Marzano, R. J. (2017). *The new art and science of teaching* (Revised and expanded ed.). Bloomington, IN: Solution Tree Press. For further information on the questioning strategies needed to engage reluctant learners, Marzano provides practical insights and information.

Wiliam, D. (2018). *Embedded formative assessment* (2nd ed.). Bloomington, IN: Solution Tree Press. For further guidelines and practical information on how to plan for and execute questioning techniques that genuinely support learning, this resource is very useful. It also provides tips on how to craft effective questions through the learning process.

Chapter 3
Self-Assessment:
Reflection and Feedback

The art of teaching is the art of assisting discovery.

—Mark Van Doren

According to D. J. Boud (1995), *student self-assessment* is defined as:

The involvement of students in identifying standards and/or criteria to apply to their work and making judgments about the extent to which they have met these criteria. (p. 12)

Rationale

Self-assessment, through reflective practice and feedback, is essential for learning growth. Hattie (2009) undertook a meta-analysis of more than eight hundred studies with the goal of identifying what really counts in student learning. What he found was that much of teachers' time is spent focusing on things that make very little difference in terms of learning achievement. He identified self-reporting as having the greatest effect size in improving student learning. Additional studies explore why this is so and what implications these findings might have on teacher practice. For example, Kuncel, Credé, and Thomas (2005) demonstrate that high school students have an accurate understanding of their achievement levels across all subjects. In addition, they found that students were also very knowledgeable about their chances for success. These findings raise some fundamental questions about the ways in which we go about our work as teachers. If students have a reasonably accurate understanding of their achievement levels and chances for success, how might we go about facilitating opportunities for students to feed this information back to the teacher? Traditionally, we test students and then provide them with feedback about their achievements. Hattie (2009) finds that it is not the feedback teachers give to students that has the largest effect on student learning outcomes but feedback students give to teachers that really counts. This understanding raises questions about how teachers go about testing and giving feedback, as it would seem that educators go about it the wrong way in many traditional practices, as shown in figure 3.1 (page 36).

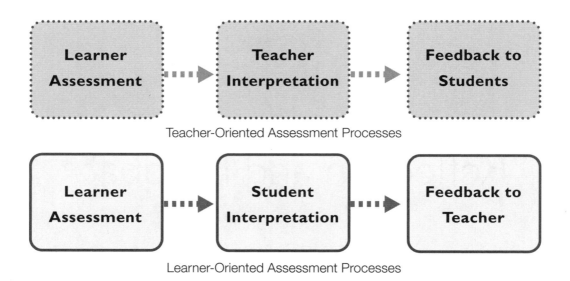

Figure 3.1: Assessment and feedback for a teacher-oriented assessment process and a learner-oriented assessment process.

It is widely acknowledged that pretesting is essential in learning design, and there has been much development in schools around ensuring students are pretested before engaging in the learning experience. While this is a positive move, we posit that this in itself is not enough. If we are pretesting and then feeding back to our students in a teacher-oriented fashion, then we may be robbing our students of the most powerful learning effect of student-oriented self-assessment processes.

Therefore, as teachers, our focus may need to be on creating opportunities for students to reflect on the learning experience by thinking about it, mulling it over, and evaluating it. Critical to this process is providing students with the opportunity to feed this information back to the teacher, who can then respond to this information by personalizing the learning experience. By working in this way, we can empower students to feel that they have control of their learning and, as a result, engage more fully in it.

In 2012, McDonald conducted a study in which a group of high school students were taught skills in self-assessment and provided with opportunities to implement these skills. Across ten secondary school settings, it was found that the students who had been taught and implemented self-assessment skills outperformed their counterparts in external examinations in all areas of the school curriculum. In addition, McDonald (2012) found that self-assessment was also useful in the following ways. These correspond with other considerations for learning that we describe in this book (they are stated in parentheses in the following list).

- Determining existing competencies (existing knowledge, chapter 13)
- Enabling students to link existing knowledge to new learning (existing knowledge and lifeworlds, chapters 13 and 10)
- Avoiding wasting time by asking students to study material they had already covered and knew (time, chapter 8)
- Supporting students to establish whether key learning goals had been met (self-assessment, this chapter)
- Assisting students in redefining self-expectations in a more positive way (expectation, chapter 9)
- Encouraging students to redefine drawbacks and challenges to setups and opportunities for innovation and progress (support and safety and desire, chapters 7 and 11)
- Empowering students in realizing that they can make things happen and that things do not just happen automatically—the power of effort (time and expectation, chapters 8 and 9)

The last point on the power of effort is critical. Effective self-assessment processes enable students to make the connection between achievement and effort rather than focusing on ability alone. While finding that the majority of students are highly competent in judging achievement levels and their chances of success, Kuncel, Credé, and Thomas (2005) find that students from minority groups, who received lower grades, are less accurate in self-estimates or self-understandings in their achievements. Hattie (2009) links this self-perception of low achievement to poor student expectations—where, often by the age of eight, students have worked out their place on the achievement ladder and see this as *out of their control*. Their experiences of poor achievement reinforce these beliefs and inevitably lead to disengagement. It is therefore an imperative to explicitly teach and foster self-assessment skills in students to enable them to identify that it is effort, rather than ability, that is essential in achievement and, as a consequence, enable them to reformulate more positive beliefs and higher expectations about themselves as learners.

As well as building student expectations, self-assessment, and feedback opportunities, teachers must ensure that the learning is pitched at a level at which students can experience success. This enables teachers and students to corroboratively design the learning experience to avoid learning experiences that are either too challenging or not challenging enough and instead create personalized learning.

In summary, by supporting students to develop self-assessment skills and providing them with the opportunities to provide feedback to the teacher, teachers can be sure to create a learning culture with:

- High expectations
- Positive self-beliefs
- High self-efficacy
- High engagement
- Empowerment of students to be active decision makers in their learning
- Collaborative relationships focused on the learning

Self-Assessment Strategies to Consider

Providing students with opportunities to self-assess and give feedback to the teacher builds a collaborative learning culture within the classroom. The following strategies can support this collaborative process.

- **Planning time for students to:**
  - Learn self-assessment skills, such as setting goals, reflecting, identifying and measuring success and effort, discussing learning with the teacher (feedback), and making active and aware decisions about learning
  - Identify the learning goals before the learning session begins
  - Reflect during and at the end of the learning experience on how they think they are doing in terms of effort and achievement (How did I do? What might I need to focus on next? What support might I need? How might I go about this?)
  - Have collaborative discussions with the teacher that focus on the learning
- **Providing students with opportunities to give feedback to the teacher about their learning achievements and needs through:**
  - Planned and informal one-to-one discussions
  - Indirect feedback with reflection templates, rubrics, learning maps, and learning continuums
- **Scaffolding student development of self-assessment skills through:**
  - Learning continuums, learning maps, and reflections (described in detail in the following sections)

While self-assessment seems to be an innate human process driven by a survival need, many students and particularly those at risk will need support initially in assessing their own learning and feeding back to the teacher. Like any behavior, the more it is practiced, the more automated it becomes. The important thing is to continually practice even if the information students initially come up with in their feedback is minimal.

Learning Continuums

Learning continuums allow students to identify their current skill level and provide them with a guide of the skills that they need to learn to move up to the next level on the continuum. Students find continuums highly engaging, as they can see and monitor their development. Continuums provide them with an end goal and help them to understand why each skill is important in reaching the end goal. In addition, they provide a framework for students to give feedback to their teachers, and they support collaborative discussions that are learning focused. Learning continuums can also be linked to benchmarked outcomes to support teachers with assessment and reporting requirements. Figure 3.2 provides an example of the first two levels of a five-level numeracy learning continuum used at Oakwood School in Victoria, Australia. In this example, students and teachers collaboratively identify the current skill level, and then the student chooses the skills he or she would like to achieve. Once achieved, the student highlights and dates the achievement and then resets his or her goals around the next learning.

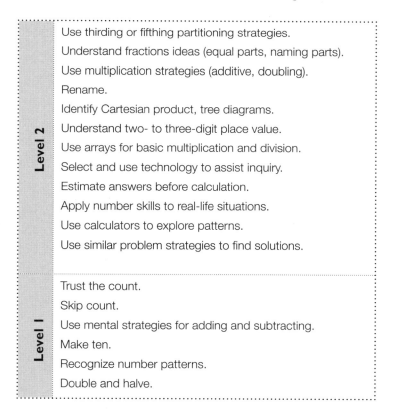

Figure 3.2: Levels 1 and 2 of a numeracy learning continuum.

Learning Maps

Learning maps provide teachers and students with a plan for how they are going to achieve the learning goals they have set. They are a collaboration between the student and the teacher based on an assessment of the student's current skill. Unlike most traditional styles of curriculum planning, where topics are covered for a certain amount of time regardless of whether each student has achieved the learning goal, the focus in the learning map is on the learning achievement, with time being the variable. Learning maps ensure that the student achieves the learning goal before moving on. They empower students to be in control of the learning and facilitate the development of self-assessment skills and collaborative learning discussion between teacher and student. There are many ways in which learning maps can be designed. Figure 3.3 (page 41) shows an example of a learning map from sixth grade.

As you can see from the example, once students achieve the learning goal, they can then date and mark it off on their learning continuum and progress to the next goal. This is a very powerful self-assessment and feedback tool that demonstrates to the student that it is effort and doing that creates learning success—not ability.

Reflections

Another form of scaffolding self-assessment skills is the use of reflections during and after the learning experience. We have found that often students are resistant to reflecting on their learning and would rather be passive than active. Maybe this is a result of their early experiences within schools where they often felt that they had little choice in or control of the learning environment. Do not be surprised if, when you introduce reflection templates, students are unable and unwilling to effectively reflect on their learning. Once again, it is about teaching students the skills of reflecting. As discussed in chapter 6, modeling can be a powerful way of teaching students the skills of reflection, so we recommend that you start by modeling the art of reflecting to the whole class, then move to reflecting with the students (group and individually), and finally move on to encouraging students to independently reflect. A template can be as simple as the following.

- Something I liked about what I did today:

- Something I found interesting:

- Something I found challenging:

- Something I wondered further about:

My Learning Plan	Reflections
Name: Elizabeth Windsor Date: March 9, 2013 Teacher: Clare Major	

My Learning Areas	Reflections
Literacy	
Reading:	
1. Use strategies to figure out more complex unfamiliar words, such as reading on, sounding out, and picking up clues from illustrations. Book: *Diary of a Wimpy Kid* Read for fifteen minutes every session. Use your reading-on and sounding-out strategies to work out any words you're not sure about.	
Literacy	
Writing:	
2. Develop a persuasive piece of writing. Explore the persuasive writing scaffold, and use it to plan out the following: "Smoking should be made illegal for people under eighteen years of age." Do you agree or disagree? 3. Use punctuation and tense to match the purpose and audience. Review the argument you gave above. What tense did you speak in? How did you use pauses, pitch, and speed to make your point? What tense should a persuasive piece of writing be in? How might you use punctuation in your writing to make your point clearer?	
Numeracy	
Numbers:	
4. Trust the count. Use the cards to practice trusting your count. 5. +/– decimal places to 0.001 Complete decimals self-assessment (number line, tense, conversion table). Check out this website to revise what we have already done: *www.khanacademy.org/math/arithmetic/arith-decimals*	

Figure 3.3: Sample learning map.

- Something I achieved today:

- What I want to achieve tomorrow:

- What I want to find out:

- What learning strategy I used today:

- The highlight for me today:

- Something I learned about myself:

Start small and build students' capacity to self-assess. With relatively simple training, interventions aimed at improving self-assessment and task-selection skills can improve student learning achievement and students' ability to self-regulate. Don't be discouraged if some of your students are resistant and produce reflections such as "I dunno." Keep going; explicitly teach self-assessment tools, and model, model, model!

Putting the Learning in Context: Sample Scenarios

Consider the following scenarios where we outline the same learning experience in two different ways: one that is inclusive of the consideration of self-assessment and one that is not.

Scenario One

Helen is an experienced teacher who enjoys working within an inquiry framework. She carefully plans an inquiry unit and puts much effort into providing a wide range of resources for her students to gain further knowledge of the topic she has introduced. She has become aware of and is feeling frustrated that some of her students are producing work that is below the standard of what she would expect and are not really engaged with the topic. Her frustration is in the fact that for the amount of effort she is putting in, the students don't seem to be responding to what she is doing. She endeavors to discuss her concerns with the underperforming students and finds that the students think one of two things.

1. That they are not really learning anything and that the work is not challenging enough (higher-achieving students)
2. That they do not really understand what they are meant to be learning and are not sure why they are doing it (lower-achieving students)

Helen recognized that both cohorts of students didn't have a clear understanding of what they were trying to achieve and what the learning goals were. Even though she had put the learning goals on the whiteboard, the learning goals seemed to be too generic to engage all the learners.

Scenario Two

Before Helen introduced the next inquiry unit, she developed a continuum of thinking skills that ranged across a number of disciplines from the grade-level standards, and asked students to self-assess where they felt their level of achievement was. She then asked students to select some learning goals from the continuum and write them on an inquiry learning map. Helen met with each student to have a discussion about what he or she had chosen to work on over the next few weeks. She developed some targeted activities that would assist students to achieve their goals and used the inquiry topic as a means for students to practice and acquire these skills. During inquiry learning time, Helen built in time for students to reflect on their learning achievements, mark on their learning map when they had achieved a goal, and feed back to her on their progress.

As a result, Helen found that her students were much more engaged in their inquiry units regardless of the topic. She also found that her knowledge of the students' learning needs increased significantly, since the time she spent with students discussing their learning goals gave the students the opportunity to provide feedback to her about what was working for them and what was not.

In the second example, Helen has carefully and deliberately used self-assessment as a tool for supporting the learner by:

- Inviting the students to assess where they are by clearly and purposefully providing a mental model of what thinking will be required to be successful
- Differentiating her support to the students through conferencing, eliciting feedback, and providing targeted activities that support their inquiries where they are needed
- Building in time for meaningful but targeted reflection to enable students to self-monitor, adjust, and respond to their learning needs in a timely and relevant manner

When Self-Assessment Is Missing

When student self-assessment, reflection, and feedback are missing, the learning environment may show the following symptoms.

- **Students who are not sure of what the learning goals are and feel lost:** Ask a colleague to visit your classroom, and invite him or her to ask your students what their learning goals are. If the students can't articulate the learning goals, what might this be telling you and your colleague? It is hard to work toward achieving a goal if you are not sure what that goal is.

- **Challenging behaviors:** If the learning goals are too challenging or not challenging enough, students may disengage through frustration and boredom. Often this will be demonstrated through challenging behaviors. In our experience, disengagement is a key indicator of a lack of self-assessment, reflection, and feedback processes.

- **Low motivation:** If students are not motivated to learn, this may be an indication that they feel the learning is done and they are not making any decisions in regard to their learning. Think of a work situation when you have been left out of a significant decision-making process that affected you. How did it make you feel? Usually, as adults, our reaction will be to disengage and feel resentful. If we feel like this as adults, imagine how our students feel in the same situation.

- **Low achievement levels and poor learning growth:** This symptom is perhaps the result of the previous three symptoms. Students who are not active in their own learning often lack the purpose and direction to succeed in their education. We can create a wonderful learning experience for our students, but if they are not a key part of the design through self-assessment, feedback, and reflection, they may choose not to engage and learn. What a huge risk we then take!

- **Teacher frustration:** There is nothing more frustrating than spending precious time developing a great unit for learning that students don't respond to. Are your students empowered to be active in the learning design? Do they set their learning goals with you collaboratively? Can they reflect and measure their own learning success? Do they have the skills? Are your students able to discuss their learning with you? Involving students in self-reflection can engage students in the learning and relieve teacher frustration in the process.

When Self-Assessment Is Evident

In a culture of self-assessment, reflection, and feedback, you will see:

- Students being clear on what they are learning and why
- High student engagement

- An emphasis on effort rather than on ability
- Powerful learning relationships between teachers and students
- Time to reflect and set goals
- Students who are able to discuss their learning
- Teachers who trust their students to self-assess and give feedback
- The use of self-assessment strategies such as learning continuums, learning maps, and reflection tools
- Students achieving actively and making decisions about their learning
- A focus on collaborative goal setting
- Learning growth for all students

Think and Reflect

1. How might you provide opportunities for your students to assess their learning?
2. How could they give feedback about their learning to you?
3. How might you ensure that planning is collaborative and that your students have a say in what they learn?
4. How might you encourage your students to set learning goals with you?
5. How could you develop self-assessment, reflection, and feedback skills in your students?
6. How might you use learning continuums and learning maps to engage students in their learning?

Supporting Ideas and Research

The following resources provide additional information and ideas you can use to further develop your knowledge of self-assessment.

Bransford, J. D., Brown, A. L., & Cocking, R. R. (2000). *How people learn: Brain, mind, experience, and school* (Expanded ed.). Washington, DC: National Academies Press. This book includes a section on feedback, reflection, and revision, providing some practical examples using technology.

Costa, A. L., & Kallick, B. (Eds.). (2008). *Learning and leading with habits of mind: 16 essential characteristics for success*. Alexandria, VA: Association for Supervision and Curriculum Development. This resource examines the role of reflection and provides some powerful strategies on how to develop a reflective classroom culture.

Covey, S. R. (1989). *The seven habits of highly effective people*. New York: Simon and Schuster. Covey examines the importance of setting goals in order to achieve, and although this book is not educationally focused, it provides evidence as to why goal setting is so critical to achievement.

Hattie, J. A. (2009). *Visible learning*. London: Routledge. Hattie provides much evidence throughout this book on the importance of giving students opportunities for self-assessment. One of his key points is that if students are given the opportunity of self-assessing, they will understand that it is their effort that counts on the achievement scale, and they will feel empowered that they can control their learning achievements through effort.

Kostons, D., van Gog, T., & Paas, F. (2012). Training self-assessment and task selection skills: A cognitive approach to improving self-regulated learning. *Learning and Instruction*, *22*(2), 121–132. This research study explores how teaching self-assessment skills can improve students' abilities to regulate their own learning.

Kuncel, N. R., Credé, M., & Thomas, L. L. (2005). The validity of self-reported grade point averages, class ranks, and test scores: A meta-analysis and review of the literature. *Review of Educational Research*, *75*(1), 63–82. This study identifies that the majority of secondary-school students are able to effectively judge their achievement levels and in addition could accurately predict their achievement level in the future. It found low-achieving students are not as effective in these skills and need some support developing these skills. This study raises questions about the feedback direction in most learning environments.

McDonald, B. (2012). *Gestalt effect of self-assessment*. West Indies: University of Trinidad and Tobago, O'Meara Campus. This published article from McDonald focuses on a research study that provides evidence that secondary-school students taught skills of self-assessment will outperform their counterparts on external examinations.

Niguidula, D. (2010). Digital portfolios and curriculum maps: Linking teacher and student work. In H. H. Jacobs (Ed.), *Curriculum 21: Essential education for a changing world* (pp. 153–162). Alexandria, VA: Association for Supervision and Curriculum Development. The author provides strategies for developing powerful feedback loops using digital portfolios and curriculum mapping.

Panadero, E. T. (2012). Rubrics and self-assessment scripts effect on self-regulation, learning and self-efficacy in secondary education. *Learning and Individual Differences*, *22*, 806–813. This study explores the effects of self-assessment rubrics and scripts on secondary-school students and found the scripts were more effective than rubrics. They also found the feedback focused on the process had the greatest effect on student achievement.

Chapter 4
Observing and Listening

> If you make listening and observation your occupation, you will gain much more than you can by talk.
>
> —Robert Baden-Powell

Observing is the art of noticing and perceiving. It involves using the senses to develop understandings and create awareness. Observing activates a student's use of his or her senses to support learning and provides a map to understanding. The key to students feeling safe, acknowledged, and valued is through a teacher's ability to both demonstrate and facilitate deep empathetic *listening* that enables everyone to walk around in one another's shoes for periods of time.

Rationale

Observation and listening are key constructs for learning, as we learn so much by what we see others do and what we hear them say. Teachers need to astutely observe and listen to learners to assist them in being able to both monitor and guide their learning progress. When teachers are conscious of the power of their own observation and spoken words, and that of their students, these constructs can be used to progress learning and raise consciousness of impact. This requires a heightened level of metacognition because the key ingredient to using this construct successfully rests in how teachers process what they observe and listen to, rather than the observation or spoken word itself. It's the interpretation of what they see and say that is critical—the inner workings of their thoughts. As Marzano and Marzano (2010) explain:

> The inner game dictates the way a teacher will behave in class, particularly in situations he or she interprets negatively. . . . Ultimately, this type of awareness and control on the part of teachers can make them more effective both in addressing difficult classroom situations and in helping students in a variety of ways. (p. 363)

Architects of learning have a raised awareness through the deliberate use of observation and listening as it relates to themselves and students. Observation and listening are inherent within each learning theory and assist all teachers to better understand what students are feeling about their learning, what is working for them, and what is challenging them. Architects of learning also powerfully use observation and listening to model key elements of the learning process with students.

Utilizing our observations and listening skills to better understand how our students are viewing their classroom and learning is key to developing empathetic dispositions as teachers. As Sousa and Tomlinson (2018) point out:

> For teacher-student relationships to be effective, teachers must be empathetic and attempt to perceive the world through their students' eyes . . . Being open and flexible helps teachers adjust to varying contexts and improves their ability to differentiate instruction and curriculum to fit their students' needs. (pp. 26–27)

Observing and Listening Strategies to Consider

The key to building observation and listening is linked to expectations and purpose for learning, and the subsequent monitoring and guiding of student learning. Using the power of observation and listening to its full extent requires you to:

- Know clearly what it is that you are looking and listening for in student work and interactions.
- Know clearly what it is that you want students to be looking for in their work.
- Model what that may look or sound like for them.
- Build reflection time purposefully and effectively into the learning experience so learners can process specifically designed reflective questions such as the following:
    - What are you noticing about the work we are doing?
    - What is your vision about how our work could look based on what I have showed you? What would you say is the best way to show your understanding?
    - What are you seeing or hearing as obstacles to your learning?
    - What did you observe or hear that helped in your learning?
    - What did you observe or hear that got in the way?
- Collect data in a nonjudgmental way that enables learners to make their own inferences and observations about it rather than hear about yours. This also helps to build effective self-assessment practices. Tell learners what you are observing in their work (without judgment—just the facts) and follow it with a meditative question to support their cognitive growth. For example, "One-fifth of our class got

above 75 percent, three-fifths got between 50 and 75 percent, and one-fifth got below 50 percent. What might be some of the reasons for these results? What might be your hunch to what we have to do to improve on this? What goals can we set as a result?"

- Collect anecdotal notes about performance, ensuring that they are connected to what learning you as a teacher are looking for, and, better still, include information from the learner in terms of how he or she is coping with the task. For instance, when recording the processes you have seen a student using to solve a number problem, note any response he or she may give you to your question that inquires into how he or she feels about the task and why. Use this as evidence for what learning dispositions the student may need support in to work successfully (for example, be more persistent when dealing with difficulty).

- Use your observations to reinforce desirable learning behaviors in your students. For example, "You have been working for five minutes, and everyone is on task. Keep up that level of focus!"

- Ask students to give insight into what they observe in a teacher or student demonstration, learning task, or teaching process. By doing this, you powerfully use the building of metacognition through the exploration of questions.

- Remember to be aware of your reaction when a potentially stressful situation escalates, such as an altercation between two students. Raising your consciousness at times such as these will ensure you remain in control of your thinking in what you are witnessing and listening to. Equally important, you will provide a calm and rational model for the students to observe and listen to.

- Use learning portfolios (where students have the opportunity to record their self-reflections) and student-led conferences (where students have the opportunity to articulate their learning) as a catalyst for observing and listening to how a student is perceiving and processing the learning experience.

Putting the Learning in Context: Sample Scenarios

Consider the following scenarios where we outline the same learning experience in two different ways: one that is inclusive of the consideration for observing and listening and one that is not.

Sanjay Dunstan is providing a lesson on the subtleties of racism through a study of the text *To Kill a Mockingbird* with his ninth-grade class.

Scenario One

The students take their seats with their copies of *To Kill a Mockingbird* and a text extract from the novel. Sanjay asks them to turn to the extract, which highlights some of the specific overtones of racist themes in the book. He redefines the term *racism* and asks his students to silently highlight evidence in the extract of racist overtones. He tells them how he wants them to explain why they would say that there is evidence of racism. He gives them twenty minutes to complete the task and returns to his desk. After the allotted time, he stops everyone and asks them to share their findings. This activity continues for ten minutes where he calls on different students with their hands up to respond. He diligently records some of the responses on the interactive whiteboard in the form of a mind map. From this, he asks groups of four students to look at the mind map and the extract to come up with key findings and evidence from the text to support the contention that the character was indeed a victim of racism. He stops everyone two minutes before the end of the lesson and reminds them that they have to finish chapter 11 before the next class.

Scenario Two

The students take their seats with their copies of *To Kill a Mockingbird* and a text extract from the novel. Sanjay explains to them that they are going to use the lesson to look for evidence to support the contention that victimization occurs in the story because of racist undertones. He asks them to observe what subtle racism might sound like by showing a YouTube clip on the interactive whiteboard. When finished, he explains how his thinking led him to believe the clip is a good illustration of racism. He then asks for their feelings about the clip and for other examples of racism they may have thought of from their own personal experiences. He redefines the term *racism* and asks his students to silently highlight evidence in the extract of racist overtones. He tells them how he wants them to be able to explain why they would say that there is evidence of racism. He gives them twenty minutes to complete the task and then roams the room interacting with the students on the extracts they are choosing, questioning them on the thinking that is leading them to their conclusions. He also answers clarifying questions as they arise. In the last ten minutes, he asks specific students to pair with other students and respond to the following instructions.

1. Take turns sharing an extract of your choice, and explain what evidence you found to suggest that it includes racist overtones.
2. Form ideas on why you think some of these characters are motivated to be racist.
3. Make one prediction you think will occur in chapter 11.

In the second example, Sanjay has carefully and deliberately used observation and listening to support the learner by:

- Providing the students the opportunity to observe and listen to his thinking on what he believes is evidence of racism when discussing the YouTube clip
- Listening to his students' experiences and connections to check for understanding and misconceptions before asking them to apply their thoughts to a task
- Observing and listening to the students' responses when they are looking for evidence of racism in the text
- Pairing students and asking that they listen intently to one another as they construct meaning together

When Observing and Listening Are Missing

When observing and listening are missing from the teacher's approach, the learning environment may show some of the following symptoms.

- Students are unclear of what thinking and processes are involved to undertake tasks successfully.
- Students may miss an opportunity to see what success looks like when working through a task.
- Teachers may misread student responses or make instructional decisions based on intuition rather than on actual evidence of what students need and feel.
- Students may see learning as something that is done to them as opposed to a process of which they can take ownership.
- The opportunity to learn how to approach complex and challenging tasks through different thinking approaches and strategies may diminish.
- Teachers may spend too much time talking at students rather than with them.

When Observing and Listening Are Evident

A learning culture where observing and listening are mindfully included will show evidence of:

- Students who connect prior knowledge to current content in discussions
- Prepared questions being shared throughout the learning by the teacher and also during the learning—this may be evident in what a teacher asks during the teaching of the lesson and then when it is recorded on a whiteboard, screen, or piece of student work

- Pausing after a teacher or student asks a question, after a teacher or student has responded to a question, and before the teacher or student asks a question
- Sound assessment practices—there may be a clear correlation between what a teacher is finding out about his or her students' understanding and how he or she is crafting questions and feedback to support them moving forward
- Teacher and students speaking in tones of voice that encourage others to think and respond
- Dialogue that focuses on growth in learning and discovery as much as on the right answer
- Purposeful questions designed to elicit specific responses, such as:
  - Knowledge retrieval
  - Individual reflections
  - Creative thinking and solutions
  - Links to other learning experiences
  - Engagement to the content
  - Connections between the learning and the life and world of the student

Think and Reflect

1. In what ways might you increase the use of the power of observation for your students?
2. When you think about your observations of your students, what might you perceive as their greatest learning needs?
3. If you were to ask your students about their observations of their learning in your class, what do you think they might say?
4. In what ways do you think they would want more support?

Supporting Ideas and Research

The following resources provide additional information and ideas you can use to further develop your knowledge of observing and listening.

Chappuis, J. (2009). *Seven strategies of assessment for learning*. Portland, OR: Educational Testing Service. In this resource, Chappuis outlines how students can close the gap through tracking, reflection, and shared learning. Observation, listening, and feeling are central to the effective use of learning journals, work samples, learning reflection, and student-led conferences.

Grift, G., & Satchwell, J. (2007). *Assessing the whole child: Creating powerful portfolios and student led conferences*. Melbourne, Australia: Hawker Brownlow Education. This book outlines how portfolios and student-led conferences can support students' metacognition. This helps teachers in their application of observation and listening skills while ensuring that the feelings of the learner are used to support learning growth.

Sousa, D. A. (2017). *How the brain learns* (5th ed.). Thousand Oaks, CA: Corwin Press. In this book, David Sousa provides ideas on how teachers can support learning through explaining the role of sensory processing. This relates specifically to the use of observation, listening, and feeling in the learning process.

Wiliam, D. (2018). *Embedded formative assessment* (2nd ed.). Bloomington, IN: Solution Tree Press. Dylan Wiliam explores and explains that there are practical ways in which educators can increase their capacity to encourage observation and listening while staying respectful to how a student feels about his or her learning.

Willis, J. (2008). *How your child learns best*. Naperville, IL: Sourcebooks Inc. Judy Willis outlines brain-friendly strategies you can use to ignite your child's learning and increase school success. Part 1 in particular will deepen your understanding of how the brain works to maximize chances for learning success relating to observing, listening, and feeling.

Chapter 5
Explicit Instruction

> Learning is not attained by chance; it must be sought for with ardor and attended to with diligence.
>
> —Abigail Adams

According to Boyles (2006), *explicit instruction* is a process that involves telling, showing, and then guiding until students obtain independence. The goal of explicit instruction is to release responsibility of learning over to the learner through carefully planned, systematic learning experiences. The instruction is direct and unambiguous (Archer & Hughes, 2011). Characterized by scaffolding (chunking the learning into digestible bites coupled with the provision of effective instructional approaches), explicit instruction ensures the learner clearly understands the instructional target and is provided with practice opportunities and feedback until he or she achieves mastery.

Rationale

There are many schools of thought about the use of explicit teaching compared with more open approaches to learning, but we don't see them as separate or mutually exclusive. When considering the construct of explicit instruction, it is important to see it as an element to your teaching repertoire as opposed to your whole approach to teaching and learning. Weber, Hierck, and Larson (2016) suggest:

> First we must embrace the genius of AND and avoid the tyranny of OR. Rigid ideologies aren't good for kids. . . . We too often settle for OR instead of designing AND solutions that will best meet the needs for all students. . . . Direct instruction pedagogies OR inquiry-based pedagogies (instead of direct instruction pedagogies AND inquiry based pedagogies). (p. 27)

Even within a more flexible learning arrangement, there is a need for explicit instruction. The key word here is *instruction*. A teacher's role within the learning journey is to instruct the learner on what to do next, what to do again, and what to refine. When a learner is truly stuck or lacks the independent learning strategies to move on in his or her learning, providing this instructional support becomes imperative. There is a strong correlation between this learning construct and modeling and exemplars, which are explored in chapter 6.

Explicit instruction is heavily influenced by the learning theory of classical behaviorist stimulus, response, and conditioning models developed by B. F. Skinner. The goal of explicit instruction is to release responsibility of learning over to the student through carefully planned, systematic learning experiences that require the teacher to have a thorough and crystal-clear understanding of the outcomes he or she is seeking. This construct is often associated with supporting students who require intervention in critical elements of the curriculum and is often best for teaching a body of content or well-defined skills, such as those in reading and mathematics.

Explicit Instruction Strategies to Consider

In any explicit instruction model, there are key attributes that serve teachers well. Drawing from these, we have broken explicit instruction into four elements to assist in understanding them in your practice. They are (1) generating attention, (2) promoting memorization of learning, (3) replicating the learning, and (4) demonstrating the learning. The following outlines each in order to assist in successfully building them into your own practice.

1. **Generate attention:** Clarify the learning purpose by guiding focused attention to the essential elements of the learning. Cater for learning preferences and abilities when instructing by repeating instructions and providing instructions in both written and verbal form. For example, in a seventh-grade lesson on the water cycle, the geography teacher shares with the students the key vocabulary of *condensation*, *precipitation*, and *evaporation*. He emphasizes to the students that they will understand these terms' meaning and relationship to one another. He introduces them through showing a game on a website that outlines the relationship and has students write the words and visually represent what they have observed.

2. **Promote memorization of learning:** Assist students in memorizing what they are learning through chunking information, providing feedback to shape or guide their learning to encourage further development and to avoid misconceptions, structuring sequential learning experiences, and teaching memory strategies such as mnemonics.

3. **Provide opportunities to replicate the learning:** Give students the opportunity to practice what they have learned. Scaffold this process by (sometimes) gradually encouraging independent performance.

4. **Provide opportunities to demonstrate the learning:** Give students the opportunity to demonstrate what they have learned to reinforce the learning and provide insight about their level of mastery or transfer. For example, the geography teacher, from the earlier example, may ask each student to work in pairs and come up with an elevator pitch that lasts no longer than thirty seconds and outlines each word's definition and the critical aspects of the words' relationship with one another. He then hears them all at the conclusion of the lesson and addresses any misconceptions and recognizes accurate responses.

In summary, a teacher should generate attention for the learning, promote ways in which students can memorize the learning, provide opportunities for students to replicate the learning, and provide opportunities for students to demonstrate the learning. The other constructs that serve teachers well when utilizing explicit instruction are through asking specific and purposeful questions, inviting self-assessment and feedback, providing models and exemplars, and monitoring use of time.

Putting the Learning in Context: Sample Scenarios

Consider the following scenarios where we outline the same learning experience in two different ways: one that is inclusive of explicit instruction and one that isn't.

In this scenario, Jane is using a ninety-minute morning block to teach her sixth-grade students how to construct a provocative introduction to a persuasive text. It became evident through the grade-level teams' common assessment that all students were having difficulty with this aspect of persuasive writing.

Scenario One

Jane explains to her students that they are going to focus on introductions to persuasive texts as their first attempt at the task showed that they were not up to standard. She introduces them to the three criteria for effective introductions.

1. They include a provocative statement. (She defines *provocative*.)
2. They include a statement of the author's position on the topic.
3. The author outlines personal and practical reasons why he or she holds this position.

She asks students to craft a new paragraph based on these three criteria in their notebooks. They are allowed to use the same topic as in their first attempt. Jane roams the room answering questions, supporting those who struggle to get started, and providing feedback on where she thinks they might need help. Early finishers are asked to read from a selection of persuasive texts from the reading box. With twenty minutes to go, she asks the students to share some of their new paragraphs with the whole class by explaining what changes they made and why. Jane is happy with the changes she has observed.

Scenario Two

Jane explains to her students that their first attempts at writing persuasive texts illustrated that they needed to work on the opening paragraph or the introduction. She explains that, while some students included some of the correct elements, on the whole, they were lacking and needed more work. She shares that what she intends for the lesson is for the students to self-assess where they think they are strong and weak and then make modifications to their opening paragraphs.

She introduces them to three things that she wants them to remember when constructing an opening paragraph.

1. They include a provocative statement. (She defines *provocative* and gives an example of a provocative statement.)
2. They include a statement of the author's position on the topic. (She provides a related example.)
3. The author outlines personal and practical reasons why he or she holds this position. (She provides specific examples.)

She then asks a student to volunteer his first-attempt paragraph. By using the interactive whiteboard, she shares her thinking with her students as she compares the elements to the student's text. She explains why she thinks he should make changes to the text and which parts. She does this for only one of the criteria.

Then the students are asked to take their work back to their tables to check the opening paragraph against the three criteria. Students are to record their reflections in their thinking journals or on the paragraph itself. After twenty minutes, Jane asks the class to share some of their observations. She records them on the whiteboard. On a new piece of paper, students are to attempt to reframe their opening paragraphs, taking into account what they just learned. With fifteen minutes to go, Jane asks students to leave out on their tables both their original and new opening paragraphs. She asks students to walk around looking at different examples, making notes on what changes students made and why. She asks for their thoughts in the last five minutes of the lesson and then makes explicit what she hears is the learning that is taking place in the specific area of constructing an opening to a persuasive text.

In the second example, Jane has carefully and deliberately used explicit instruction as a tool for supporting the learner:

- By generating attention. This was done through explicitly providing a rationale for the focus on the lesson, sharing criteria of the learning, and giving examples of what the criteria mean in relation to learners' own work.

- By supporting the memorization of key learning through having the learners apply the criteria to their own work and discussing those reflections with the whole class after using an actual example from one of the students.
- By building in time for replicating the learning through rewriting the paragraph anew.
- By demonstrating the learning through assessing other students' work based on the criteria. This is also supported by asking the students to note what they notice and what the reasons are for their reflections. She also leaves herself enough time at the conclusion of the lesson to check for understanding and to address the progress they have made.

When Explicit Instruction Is Missing

When explicit instruction is missing from the teacher's approach, the learning environment may show some of the following symptoms.

- Learners are unclear of what thinking and processes are involved to undertake the task successfully.
- Learners may miss an opportunity to see what successful thinking looks and sounds like when working through a task.
- Learners find it difficult to get started on a task or apply what the teacher has just explained.
- Learners perceive or feel that the teacher doesn't really explain things properly.
- Learners struggle to apply new approaches to challenging learning tasks, leading to a lack of growth in their learning and the subsequent results.
- Teachers tend to spend time discussing what has to be done with little focus on why learners are doing it and how.
- Teachers and learners make limited connections between the content of the lesson and their personal experiences.
- More time is spent on talking about the task than is spent doing it.

When Explicit Instruction Is Evident

A learning culture that includes explicit instruction that is mindfully applied will show evidence of:

- Students who engage in the task and become aware of what they need to replicate or practice in order to get better
- Students who have tools and mental models for working through more complex tasks

- Students with a working understanding of what it looks like and sounds like to be successful within a specific task, assignment, or process
- Dialogue that centers explicitly on the learning and what is intended to be understood
- Plenty of opportunities for:
  - Paying attention to the learning
  - Developing strategies to remember key aspects to the learning
  - Applying the learning though guided practice
  - Using the thinking and concrete models to support learning (for example, posters, charts, recorded dialogue, work samples, sharing of internal thinking processes, and exemplars)

Think and Reflect

1. In what ways might you increase your use of explicit instruction for your students?
2. When you think about explicit instruction and your students, what do you perceive as their greatest learning needs?
3. If you were to ask your students about the explicit instructions they would most benefit from, what do you think they might say?

Supporting Ideas and Research

The following resources provide additional information and ideas you can use to further develop your knowledge of explicit instruction.

Archer, A. L., & Hughes, C. A. (2011). *Explicit instruction: Effective and efficient teaching*. New York: Guilford Press. This very practical resource contains detailed examples and explanations of explicit teaching practices, including lesson plans.

Danielson, C. (2007). *Enhancing professional practice: A framework for teaching* (2nd ed.). Alexandria, VA: Association for Supervision and Curriculum Development. In Domain 3: Instruction, Carol Danielson outlines indicators for how effective teachers communicate with their students. This supports the concept of explicit instruction as we have defined it.

Hattie, J. A. (2009). *Visible learning*. London: Routledge. John Hattie summarizes some interesting work on direct instruction (pages 204–207) and makes an important distinction between the very effective direct instruction and didactic teaching. He articulates well the elements of direct instruction.

Marzano, R. J. (2007). *The art and science of teaching: A comprehensive framework for effective instruction*. Alexandria, VA: Association for Supervision and Curriculum Development. In this comprehensive study and explanation of research-based instructional strategies, Robert Marzano outlines many ways in which educators can be explicit in instruction. He provides research and tips to ensure that students understand what teachers want them to learn and how to develop generative knowledge.

Parker, M., & Hurry, J. (2007). Teachers' use of questioning and modelling comprehension skills in primary classrooms. *Educational Review, 59*(3), 299–314. This research study found that modeling and questioning practices are more effective if teachers explicitly teach students what they are doing while they are doing it. The key is the explicit teaching that goes on while demonstrating a skill or strategy.

Chapter 6
Modeling and Exemplars

Tell me, and I forget. Show me, and I remember. Involve me, and I learn.

—Chinese Proverb

Modeling is the art of showing something explicitly in order to increase understanding. It activates the senses and creates a working example in which students can anchor their understanding. *Exemplars* are models of excellence that depict expectations and possibilities for students. They provide a benchmark for both teacher and student expectations.

Rationale

If we want our students to be successful, effective teachers provide students with the opportunity to see what it looks like to be both successful and unsuccessful, providing the opportunity to learn through investigating similarities and differences. They model behaviors that support learning success and demonstrate thinking processes and strategies to support students' work through complexities and challenges in their learning. Providing learners with opportunities to interact with models may greatly increase their chances of learning successfully and assist in the practicing and deepening of their understanding (Marzano, 2017).

To model process, explicit language, instructions, thinking, behaviors, and work exemplars is to give our learners something to hold on to—a mental model that they otherwise might not have. Essential to effective modeling, teachers ensure they break down their explanations of skills, processes, and strategies into smaller parts and express their thoughts aloud, giving students a window into their thinking.

Exemplars usually involve the sharing of a work sample or finished product. Sometimes referred to as worked examples, they demonstrate the expected learning in relation to the criteria for that standard and ensure students get the opportunity to see what proficiency would look like if they were to be successful. Students know the steps required to achieve success through the teacher's explanation of how they relate to the exemplar being shared. An exemplar will only be powerful when it is modeled by the teacher effectively, hence the interrelationship between them both.

Both modeling and exemplars are linked to observational learning or imitation (critical to behaviorist learning theory) and require the teacher and students to demonstrate what is to be learned, what is being learned, and what has been learned. It provides a visual and auditory pathway for students to rehearse, reinforce, and revise their learning on the way to mastery.

Modeling and Exemplar Strategies to Consider

To be able to model something or even demonstrate a process, you first need to be clear about what you are modeling, how it might impact on learning, and where it relates to the learning objectives. Some possible strategies to support modeling and exemplars include the following.

- **Representing learning through different modalities:** You could introduce a concept, such as multiplication, visually (for example, with equations, arrays, or large dots), auditorily (for example, with spoken tables, sums, or real-life problems), or kinesthetically (for example, by having students form groups or manipulate counters into groups).

- **Incorporating cooperative groups into class:** Marzano (2017) explains this strategy is one that "involves a) designing structures for group and individual accountability b) providing ongoing coaching of students c) specifying clear roles and responsibilities for all group members d) using a variety of grouping criteria and grouping structures" (p. 62). This helps students see the way other students work through complexity, solve problems, and approach tasks. It also will often provide them with gaps in their knowledge in the safety of a smaller group.

- **Modeling thinking out loud:** Think-alouds provide an insight into the teacher's thinking through explicitly explaining how he or she works through a task. This shows students how to work through a problem or learning task. It demonstrates what the process looks like, what conversations will and won't sound like, and what questions students should develop. This is done through thinking aloud and visually representing, through charts, posters, and student work, what is expected in terms of thinking, content, presentation, knowledge, and so on.

- **Using social thinking:** Social thinking is the teacher's ability to ensure students' voices are used as a lever to help others learn from them through a social context. It encourages students to model their thinking, predominantly through demonstration and conversation opportunities.

- **Providing opportunities for feedback:** Teacher-to-student, student-to-student, and student-to-teacher feedback provides models for further improvement by showing what others think good work looks like or what worked for them.

- **Using digital avenues to demonstrate the learning students should master:** Avenues such as YouTube and podcasts are providing teachers with many opportunities to engage students in observing models for them in their learning.

- **Maximizing peer teaching:** This enables students to learn from one another within a context that they may more readily understand. Often students will use language and have developed a rapport that is easier for their peers to understand. They are more aligned to each other's stage of development than adults are and so can be powerful activators of learning for one another.

- **Providing successful and unsuccessful models of work:** Students can compare and reflect on the models, building criteria for success and a mental model of what it might look like to achieve the learning.

- **Planning for key learning that may need modeling:** Teachers identify opportunities during the curriculum design process to explicitly build in models and exemplars. Typically, this key learning involves the introduction of new concepts, complex processes requiring deeper explanations, and the practicing of concepts, strategies, and processes.

Putting the Learning in Context: Sample Scenarios

Consider the following scenario where we outline the same learning experience in two different ways: one that is inclusive of modeling and exemplars and one that isn't.

A highly regarded high school was reviewing the pass rates for twelfth-grade psychology students and found that, although the pass rates were good, there was a high dropout rate. Upon further inquiry, they were perplexed to find that those who were dropping out were students who had performed quite well in eleventh grade. Concerned, the head of the department, Stuart Little, did some further analysis and discovered that most of the students dropping out attended the same class run by colleague Barry Hart. Stuart decided to observe Barry's class to see if he could identify what was happening and why, and then observed Chris Pure's class (another twelfth-grade teacher) to see if there were any differences.

Scenario One: Mr. Hart's Class

Barry welcomed the students as they came into the room and started the class on time. He articulated the goal of the session, which was primarily to revise the content of the last lesson on the role of the brain in mental processes and behavior, with a specific focus on the relationship between the nervous systems as communication systems. He spent twenty minutes revisiting the theory and then presented the students with a set of practical problems to solve, designed to illustrate what the brain does when confronted with problems. He provided them with an answer sheet to check their own understanding as they progressed. (The answer sheet had the answers only and showed no work.) He gave his students the next thirty minutes to work on their problem sets and encouraged them to ask for help if they needed it. As students finished the problem set, they were permitted to leave the class.

Scenario Two: Dr. Pure's Class

Chris welcomed the students as they came into the room and started the class on time. He articulated the goal of the session, which was primarily to revisit the content of the last lecture on the relationship between the brain and thought processes and behavior. Chris spent the first five minutes recapping the lecture briefly, gave out the practice problem sets, and then provided students with a model of how to work through a problem. As he went through the model, he articulated what he was doing and why. He then asked the students to attempt the first five problems, which were similar to the one he had just modeled. After ten minutes, he brought the class back together and asked individual students to model on the whiteboard how they had solved the problems.

He asked the individual students to talk the class through what they were writing. For the next twenty minutes, he allowed students to work independently but made himself available to work with a small group of students who felt they needed further demonstration. During the last ten minutes, he handed out an answer sheet complete with all the work—so that students could check their understanding—and summarized what they had learned as a result of doing the problems.

In the second example, Chris has carefully and deliberately used modeling and exemplars as a tool for supporting the learner by:

- Providing the students with an actual model of how to work through the problems they were about to attempt. He did so not just by sharing what to do but through thinking aloud why he was working it through in that way.
- Providing the students with the opportunity to model for one another how they went about solving the problems they were given.
- Making himself available to the students to demonstrate further should they become stuck in their approaches to solving the problems set out in their work. He was explicit on the type of support he would provide.

When Modeling and Exemplars Are Missing

When modeling and exemplars are not a key element within the learning environment, the following symptoms may be evident.

- **Misconceptions and misunderstandings:** If individual students are displaying errors consistently in their work, they may need more explicit modeling. This is also the case if you see a consistent error across a whole class around a particular concept. The concept may need more explicit modeling.

- **Challenging behavior:** If modeling is absent or not explicit enough, students may avoid applying themselves to a task that they are unsure of to remove the risk of exposure. In addition, confusion can lead to frustration for students, which often leads to acting out. Avoidance and frustration are two key behaviors to watch out for as an indicator that more explicit modeling may be required.

- **Low motivation:** If students are not motivated to learn, this may be an indication that they are feeling unsure about what they are meant to be doing. It is hard to feel enthusiastic about something you are confused about.

- **Teacher frustration:** If you feel as though you can't seem to get through to students, that it doesn't matter what you say—they just don't get it—you might not be sharing your thinking with students so that they get a clear picture of the learning.

When Modeling and Exemplars Are Evident

When modeling and exemplars exist within the learning environment, the following may be evident.

- Learners become clear about the learning process.
- Learners are highly engaged, and the quality of task completion is high.
- Learners feel confident that, when they ask a question about the learning, they will be shown a way to move forward and receive a verbal explanation.
- Learners are able to identify and articulate what part of the learning they are having difficulty with rather than making global statements such as "I can't do this."
- Learners can show others how they went about their learning.
- Learners self-assess their learning processes and refine them as they go.
- All students show learning growth.

Think and Reflect

1. When you reflect on your teaching, when do you think you use modeling powerfully to support learning? When might you need to?

2. What might be some of the options open to you to use modeling, specifically during the teaching of a lesson, unit, or course?

3. When do you feel that your students would like to see more modeling, and in what areas of their learning?

Supporting Ideas and Research

The following resources provide additional information and ideas you can use to further develop your knowledge of modeling and exemplars.

Berk, L. E., & Winsler A. (1995). *Scaffolding children's learning: Vygotsky and early childhood education*. NAEYC Research Into Practice, Vol. 7. This issue in the series examines Vygotsky's work on the process of scaffolding that was based largely on modeling.

Bransford, J. D., Brown, A. L., & Cocking, R. R. (2000). *How people learn: Brain, mind, experience, and school* (Expanded ed.). Washington, DC: National Academies Press. This book uses examples of software programs, providing simulations of complex models that students can manipulate to develop their understanding. The emphasis is on how models are integrated into the classroom to ensure effective learning outcomes (rather than on the models themselves).

Costa, A. L., & Kallick, B. (Eds.). (2008). *Learning and leading with habits of mind: 16 essential characteristics for success*. Alexandria, VA: Association for Supervision and Curriculum Development. This resource examines the role of reflection and provides some powerful modeling strategies on how to develop a reflective classroom culture.

Parker, M., & Hurry, J. (2007). Teachers' use of questioning and modelling comprehension skills in primary classrooms. *Educational Review*, 59(3), 299–314. This research study looks at the way modeling can be used to improve literacy skills. One of the findings of the study is that, for modeling to gain maximum learning effect, it is vitally important for the teacher to be explicit about the modeling. It found that although teachers were modeling a reading strategy, the majority were not explicit with the students about what they were doing and as a result the modeling was ineffective.

Sempowicz, T., & Hudson P. (2011). Analysing mentoring dialogues for developing a preservice teacher's classroom management practices. *Australian Journal of Teacher Education*, 36(8), 1–16. This study recognizes the importance of providing effective modeling of school behavior management plans to support preservice teachers to develop effective management practices. Inexperienced teachers were more able to develop effective behavior management practices if they had seen effective modeling.

Sousa, D. A. (2017). *How the brain learns* (5th ed.). Thousand Oaks, CA: Corwin Press. Sousa outlines how the discovery of mirror neurons in the brain has led some neuroscientists to the belief that we are wired to learn through watching and listening to others. This may explain the power and role of modeling, and the development of empathy in learning.

Chapter 7
Support and Safety

> True teachers are those who use themselves as bridges over which they invite their students to cross; then, having facilitated their crossing, joyfully collapse, encouraging them to create their own.
>
> —Nikos Kazantzakis

Within the learning environment, *support* refers to the efforts made to ensure learning success through carefully planned learning experiences that are personalized to suit the learner's needs. This process is often referred to as *scaffolding* and applies to the learner's cognitive, emotional, and social dimensions. Scaffolding enables a student to feel safe in the learning environment. The learning environment has *safety* when it has a culture in which learners feel protected from harm or damage while being encouraged to explore and take risks.

Rationale

Any learning experience is enhanced through both informal and more formalized support structures. As architects of the learning experience, it is important that teachers recognize key moments and approaches that they can use to help students more successfully interact with their learning. In the classroom, teachers need to consider their role in supporting learners, how students can support other learners, and how learners support themselves in a physically and psychologically safe environment.

Many students we have spoken to talk about how isolated they can feel from their learning. One boy interviewed for *Assessing the Whole Child* (Grift & Satchwell, 2007) stated in response to a question about what contributed to his improvement that he:

> Had to keep going . . . there was no one there backing him up and he just had to talk to himself and tell himself to push through. The whole world was saying he couldn't do it but he had to. What choice does he have?

It was evident he was drawing from every internal resource he had to break through a feeling of isolation and anxiety.

While this may be an extreme example, the student's perception of his learning experience still highlights the impact a perceived lack of support can have on the internal thinking processes of a student, whether that be from home, school, or a combination of both. Teachers who are able to construct classroom environments that provide high levels of support and safety ultimately become more successful. Sousa and Tomlinson (2010) describe nine assumptions and beliefs that sit behind what effective teachers do to guide their practice and create the safe and supportive environment students seek. These teachers believe the following.

1. They have a lifelong impact.
2. Classrooms must feel safe and secure.
3. All students want to succeed.
4. The social-emotional needs of students must be met.
5. Empathy is very important.
6. Students should feel a sense of ownership in their education.
7. Teachers should identify and reinforce each student's areas of competence.
8. Teachers should address fears of failure and humiliation.
9. Discipline is a teaching process. (pp. 19–26)

Interestingly, they found that providing a safe and secure classroom, from a neuroscience perspective, may open neural pathways to learning and maximize the potential for students to take greater risks in their learning. Complex cognitive processes are often suspended when the student detects an unsupportive or unsafe environment and the subsequent confusion, anger, or fear can then overcome rational thought, leading to less conducive learning behaviors.

You may have experienced the difference between what it is like to learn in an environment that feels safe and one that doesn't. Most students, unfortunately, experience situations in which they do not feel completely free to speak their minds and learn without fear of ridicule. A supportive and safe classroom is one where students feel it is OK to:

• Make mistakes
• Contribute to discussions without fear of ridicule or personal judgment
• Receive feedback that supports the growth of the work or learning
• Provide feedback to others to support the growth of the work or learning
• Be themselves
• Think outside of the box
• Talk to the teacher, each other, and themselves
• Ask questions of the teacher and other students
• Reflect and assess their own work, as well as contribute to the assessment of others' work
• Be fuzzy in their learning in terms of Vygotsky, Hanfmann, and Vakar's (2012) zone of proximal development (not too easy but not too complex)
• Set some personal goals in relation to the work

Support and Safety Strategies to Consider

Some of the ways we might support learners and create safety through the learning experience fall into three categories: cognitive learning support, behavioral learning support, and structural support.

Cognitive Learning Support

Cognitive learning support relates to what the teacher does to ensure his or her students learn both the what and the how of a subject or discipline area. Cognitive learning support includes the following.

- **Time for reflection and learning consolidation within the lesson or unit structure:** *Learning consolidation* refers to the times a teacher uses to reinforce the key understandings of a learning experience with and for students. It is the opportunity teachers take to ensure the learning is made prominent throughout the learning experience. It includes spending time talking to students about their learning and providing space for responses to questions that have arisen through the learning, as discussed in chapter 2.

- **Formally building metacognition into the learning process:** Metacognition in this construct relates to the ability of the teacher to illuminate for learners what thinking is assisting them to learn something successfully. It enables the students to discover as much about the process of learning as they can rather than just what they are learning. For example, you might ask students to develop portfolios or different thinking structures, such as Edward de Bono's (2009) six thinking hats, to encourage learners to consider what thinking is assisting them and what thinking might be getting in the way. To highlight this strategy, consider the teacher who at the conclusion of a lesson asks his students to reflect on the learning though the green hat (focuses on creativity; the possibilities, alternatives, and new ideas— it's an opportunity to express new concepts and new perceptions). Students offer suggestions on how they might apply their learning to other contexts or future work through the targeted and open-ended questions of the teacher.

- **Graphic organizers:** These tools are effective for supporting thinking in the classroom, provided they have been intentionally matched to the purpose of the learning and that the tool guides students to the correct thinking or results. For example, students can use a Venn diagram to find similarities and differences between two characters in a fictional book. Or they can use a placemat, a strategy in which students individually and silently add their thoughts to a task or topic on a shared piece of paper and then share and elaborate on their ideas in a small-group context.

Behavioral Learning Support

Behavioral learning support relates to what teachers do to ensure their students learn acceptable and productive behaviors that support learning and that keep learning as the focus. Behavioral learning support includes the following.

- **Using reinforcement:** For example, this may involve articulating what is working and not working, recognizing misconceptions and challenging them, and publicly articulating key thinking that is supporting the meeting of learning objectives.
- **Shaping learning behavior:** This is done by rewarding either extrinsically (stickers, charts, stars, ticks, grades, and so on) or intrinsically (with specific praise, observations, and self-assessment) the success of learners as they evolve through the learning journey.
- **Collaboratively developing student-directed learning goals:** After developing the goals, students have the opportunity to self-assess and measure their own learning as means of intrinsic motivation and ownership of their learning journey.

Structural Support

Structural support relates to the operational elements teachers focus on in their support of student learning. They are key ingredients to providing a safe place to learn. Structural support strategies to increase levels of learning may include the following.

- Providing examples of how the learning might look (modeling and exemplars).
- Asking students who are succeeding to share their thinking with others.
- Providing examples of process, product, or content.
- Providing alternative ways of thinking or approaching a task for students who are experiencing difficulty.
- Using meditative questions such as "When you think about what is difficult, which aspects of the task seem to be stopping you?"
- Providing clear instructional modeling. For example, "This is how you do it," "This is what you need to think about as you do it," "This is how John tackled it," and so on.
- Providing an easier or more difficult task to scaffold the learning to individual learners.
- Giving feedback to learners through one-to-one conferencing either informally or formally that centers on the work and recognizes:
  - Areas for celebration
  - Areas for strengthening
  - Areas of interest
  - Areas for further investigation

- Exploring how the teacher might continue to support the learner.
- Explicitly linking the work to the learning objectives.
- Expressing positive expectations in language that is rich in presuppositions, such as "I know you can," "When you've been successful before," and "You know how you did this part correctly."
- Using social learning support, such as:
  - Peer teaching, which can be used in smaller groups to enable learners to hear thinking from different perspectives
  - Classroom experts or consultants who can assist in areas where they have a deeper level of knowledge, skill, and application
  - Cooperative learning strategies, where each member of a group is given an explicit role to support the process of collaborative learning—for example, each member of a group is assigned a different role, such as summarizer, speaker, recorder, or questioner, and is actively involved in and supports the group
- Developing a class learning plan that clearly articulates expectations for learning and behavior, co-constructed by the teacher and students. Co-creation of such structures provides security and sets up a positive learning culture in which students can feel safe to explore, create, and innovate. (See the appendix for examples of learning plans from a K–12 classroom.)
- Developing relationships through being intentional in getting to know a student's interests and background, coupled with a curiosity on what is going on in his or her lifeworld.
- Having fun by promoting times for social conversation, fun, and frivolity to build relationships and personal understandings.
- Being aware by taking the temperature of your students—observing when things are not quite right and respectfully acknowledging those observations to each student in a private and confidential manner. For example, "Alice, I have noticed that you are finding it hard to concentrate at the moment. Is there any way I can support you more? Is there anything you would like to chat about?"
- Celebrating progress through effective feedback, not only about academic progress but also for effort, persistence, getting along with others, managing conflict, or taking on difficult challenges.
- Creating an inviting, ordered physical environment by making your classroom a place that screams out, "Kids learn and laugh within these walls!" For example, post student work on the walls—both drafts and final products. Create spaces where students can be part of the physical running of the class and where they feel part of the reason why the class operates effectively.
- Providing forums for problem solving such as regular class meetings, student-led conferences, individual meetings, and restorative processes where student capacity is built to resolve conflict.

- Empowering students by encouraging them, in collaboration with their teacher, to set learning goals, reflect on their progress, and develop strategies to support future learning.
- Being transparent about assessments that will measure student work so that learners feel secure about the learning expectations.

Putting the Learning in Context: Sample Scenarios

Consider the following scenarios where we outline the same learning experience in two different ways: one that is inclusive of support and safety and one that isn't.

Kerry is working with her eleventh-grade history class in preparation for their end-of-year examinations. Over a fifty-minute period, she has freed up the session for them so that they can focus on asking questions and accessing information from areas on their practice test that they struggled with.

Scenario One

The students file in and take their seats. Kerry hands out the practice test with identified areas of priority for them to focus on. She has placed focus readings and information summaries in the key concept areas covered in their practice test on a side bench in the room. She explains that she wants students to go over the test and then take corresponding key concept material from the bench and read through it, using the highlight-and-record technique she taught them previously. She lets them know that they can come and ask her any clarifying questions that they may have, but that they should not approach her at her desk because she is marking some other work of theirs and they should ensure they have checked with someone else before asking her. She finishes the lesson by asking each student to share an insight he or she has made as a result of his or her study. During the lesson, she warns two students to focus when they lose concentration and also sends one student out for repeatedly not following her directions as part of the whole-school process for managing behavior.

Scenario Two

As students enter the classroom, Kerry checks in with a few of them by making a joke about their appearance that morning. She comments that the biggest challenge she has is to keep them awake, going by the look of them! She explains that the purpose of the session is to support them in developing deeper understandings of misconceptions they have based on the information from their practice assessment. She has placed focus readings and information summaries in the key concept areas covered in their practice test on a side bench in the room. She explains that she wants students to go over the test and then take corresponding key concept material from the bench and read through it using the highlight-and-record technique she taught them previously. Prior to this task, she shares with them some things she noticed that she believes they all need to know in order to be successful. She presents it as a humorous mnemonic, but most students don't laugh. She challenges them to see if they can come up with something better in five minutes. She instructs them that they can share some of their mnemonics at the conclusion of the lesson, suggesting that she won't be holding her breath, though.

The students go through their test and access relevant information from the bench. Throughout the process, Kerry roams the class and talks with the students about their misconceptions of content, explaining different ways to help them understand. From time to time she stops the whole class to share an insight with the whole group, as she believes it will help them all. Kerry reiterates her belief that they can all be highly successful in their examination and asks them to take home what they have started for further study. She reminds them that there is no compensation for persistence and commitment to their study and that she knows they have what it takes to designate time to doing this. She shares a correlating brief story of when she was in a similar situation during her teaching degree and what she had to do. She finishes the lesson with some of her students' attempts at mnemonics from earlier.

In the second example, Kerry has deliberately used strategies from the construct of support and safety to support the learning by:

- Connecting with individual students and being deliberate in her use of humor.
- Engaging with students when they are working to demonstrate interest, support, and a willingness to be a resource for them.
- Sharing personal anecdotes as way of modeling that she understands the challenges and what it takes to overcome them from a subjective perspective. This sends the message that she understands learning and is approachable to the students.
- Sending the message that she believes in their capabilities and knows that they can and will be successful.

When Support and Safety Are Missing

When support and safety are missing from the teacher's approach, the learning environment may show some of the following symptoms.

- Higher levels of behavior problems for disengaged learners
- Fewer questions coming from students in relation to their learning
- Students experiencing lower levels of learning success
- Certain students monopolizing classroom conversations to the learning detriment of others
- Inconsistent expectations and follow-through in terms of both learning and behavioral processes and approaches
- Students perceiving the teacher as having favorites
- The teacher developing high levels of frustration in terms of student behavior and understanding
- The teacher finding it difficult to separate the behavior from the student
- Increased incidents of bullying—both overt and covert
- Students learning more through fear of consequences than through a love of learning

When Support and Safety Are Evident

A learning culture where safety and support are mindfully considered and applied may show evidence of:

- A higher level of interaction centered on learning between students and teachers, and among students
- More humor in the classroom
- Higher student attendance levels
- A reduction in bullying incidents and behavioral disruptions to learning
- A greater number of questions being asked by a greater proportion of students
- An environment that engages in challenging conversations in terms of addressing both learning and behaviors
- Higher student achievement levels
- Greater peer support centering more on learning growth rather than relentless academic and social competition

Think and Reflect

1. In what ways might you support learning for all your students?
2. What is your sense of the strategies your students most value in supporting their learning?
3. As you think about the times you have learned things deeply, what were the key support functions that worked for you?
4. What might be some indicators for you that your support is effective in helping your students learn?
5. In what ways might you build on the safe learning environment that you are implementing?
6. As you think about times in your learning when you felt safe and supported, what might have been some of the factors that led to this feeling?
7. When you picture your classroom environment, what is your sense of what is working and what might need revisiting?

Supporting Ideas and Research

The following resources provide additional information and ideas you can use to further develop your knowledge of support and safety.

Berk, L. E., & Winsler A. (1995). *Scaffolding children's learning: Vygotsky and early childhood education*. NAEYC Research Into Practice, Vol. 7. This article examines Vygotsky's work on the process of scaffolding to support student learning.

Danielson, C. (2007). *Enhancing professional practice: A framework for teaching* (2nd ed.). Alexandria, VA: Association for Supervision and Curriculum Development. In Domain 2: The classroom environment, Carol Danielson outlines specific elements for providing a safe and supportive environment, including creating an environment of respect and rapport, establishing a culture for learning, managing classroom procedures, managing student behavior, and organizing physical space.

Marzano, R. J. (2007). *The art and science of teaching: A comprehensive framework for effective instruction*. Alexandria, VA: Association for Supervision and Curriculum Development. In this comprehensive study and explanation of research-based instructional strategies, Robert Marzano outlines many ways in which we can build a learning environment conducive to high levels of learning. In particular, he explores how we might do this by outlining classroom routines, procedures, rules, and the explicit building of relationships.

Seligman, M. E. P. (2011). *Flourish*. New York: Free Press; and Seligman, M. E. P. (1995). *The optimistic child*. Boston: Houghton Mifflin. In his pioneering work, Martin Seligman defines and describes the impact that positive psychology can have on our well-being and happiness, and therefore the capacity to learn at higher levels.

Tomlinson, C. A. (2003). *Fulfilling the promise of the differentiated classroom*. Alexandria, VA: Association for Supervision and Curriculum Development. This, as with many of Carol Tomlinson's other books, provides many useful classroom strategies that, once implemented, increase the chances of students feeling safe and supported in the learning environment.

Sousa, D. A., & Tomlinson, C. A. (2018). *Differentiation and the brain* (2nd ed.). Bloomington, IN: Solution Tree Press. This book provides information on the neuroscience and practical ideas effective teachers apply to create safe and supportive classrooms, and an ability to cater for a variety of students from different contexts.

Chapter 8
Time

A process cannot be understood by stopping it. Understanding must move with the flow of the process, must join it and flow with it.

—Frank Herbert

Time is a critical dimension within the learning environment. Its importance is not just that it exists and helps us to chart our day but that it is a variable that teachers can manipulate to support student learning. We cannot make the day longer, but we can increase or decrease the amount of time we give to students to support their learning. In the learning context, time is a variable that can be manipulated to ensure it doesn't become a constraint to learning.

Rationale

We all understand the power time has on learning, but we still feel compelled to stick to the timetable. In fact, many of our curriculum-planning processes lend themselves to rushing through the teaching of concepts, knowledge, and skills before students have really understood what they might mean. Until we change the way we plan and move away from the week-by-week inflexible approach to planning, we are in danger of leaving students behind in their learning. Moreover, we make it difficult to let learning lead the way, choosing instead to stick to an approach where teaching leads the way.

If we want to differentiate our instruction by need and respond to students in the moment, then teachers must create the opportunity for more flexibility in regard to time. Hattie (2009) identifies the importance of time on task, emphasizing that time on task is not merely practicing a skill; it is the deliberate concentration on improving performance. This is difficult given the amount of material that teachers feel they have to cover, but it's essential if learning, and not teaching, is to take center stage. Often, teachers move from task to task to cover the curriculum as opposed to applying deliberate concentration principles and encouraging students to uncover the curriculum. When there is no flexibility, teachers can fall victim to anxiety from the following outcomes.

- **They haven't got it:** When students aren't where they should be because of curriculum content, pressure, and time. It feels like we are saying to students, "Listen, we know you don't understand fractions yet, but Mrs. Smith will work on that with you next year. We have to move on to area and perimeter."
- **They've already got it, but . . . :** When students understand but we haven't provided enough time for them to develop more abstract and lateral applications of the knowledge to understand key concepts in a deeper sense. This is at the expense of engaging them in areas where they have found genuine interest and engagement in the learning.
- **They were just getting it:** When students have just grasped the concept and, with extra time to practice, would have been more likely to transfer their understanding to long-term memory.

If time is so critical to the success of the learning experience, then it is time schools did things differently. In high schools, timetables have been driving the learning over a long period of time. In elementary schools, there can be too many disconnected programs that get in the way of embedding significant time for key concepts, knowledge, and skills, hijacking the students' genuine chances to learn deeply. This can be addressed through meeting the challenges of some of the culprits for this, such as the overcrowded curriculum. Through prioritizing curriculum and developing clarity as to what needs to be taught, educators can better address the problems associated with timetables, for example.

Viv White, former director for the Australian National Schools Network, is an advocate for what she has called the *slow schools movement*—the ability for a school to take charge of what it implements through having a clear vision and mission and aligning efforts to achieve these. In a sense, this means filtering out the programs and processes that create busy but ineffectual schools. While she is talking about this in terms of systemic and whole-school change, in our view, the same should be seriously addressed in the building of programs and timetables that directly impact classroom learning.

It's the allocation of time within a school and classroom, based on the key priority of having a relentless focus on learning, that is critical. As Rick DuFour and his colleagues (2016) point out:

> When something is truly a priority in an organization, people do not hope it happens; they develop and implement systematic plans to ensure that it happens. For example, if the leadership team was committed to creating a collaborative culture, they could take steps to organize teachers into teams, build time for collaboration into the contractual workday, develop protocols and parameters to guide the work of teams, and so on. (p. 35)

Time Strategies to Consider

As teachers, we need to provide space in the program for learners to engage in the three Ps: practice, practice, and more practice. While some students need more time to practice than others, it is imperative that we spend considerable time immersing students in key concepts so that they develop generative knowledge. This may mean that collaborative teams need to decide what the key concepts (or essential learnings) are—or, as Larry Ainsworth (2003) describes them, *power standards*.

If we don't reprioritize and reorganize our time in lessons to provide the most time for learning key concepts, using assessments in formative ways can become extremely problematic. For example, providing feedback is important, but it's easy to forgo it when we feel we have too much content to cover and not enough time to cover it. This means that, in turn, we don't give ourselves the opportunity to genuinely talk with our students about their work, listen to students talk about their learning, or even spend the time processing what the work has taught us. Self-assessment and peer assessment are often shuffled to the end of a unit or lesson, due to lack of time, rather than interwoven into the learning journey as an integral part of the process. Approaches teachers can take to use time effectively include the following.

- Prioritizing high-leverage standards in areas deemed most important by the state, district, school, community, or society, and delving into those deeply.

- Reviewing the existing timetable and eradicating any programs, events, or ceremonies that do not contribute to the essential learning so students have greater chances to connect to their learning experiences.

- Resisting the urge to plan week by week with set activities, as this takes away from being able to flexibly respond within the learning experience. Instead, plan your teaching around key concepts, knowledge, and skills. A series of disjointed activities without the time to learn deeply erodes the possibility for acquiring generative knowledge.

- Integrating key interdisciplinary learning into the timetable authentically. It is common to see elementary programs with literacy blocks in the morning, mathematics in the middle block, and integrated time in the afternoon. Instead, perhaps the whole day could be categorized as *integrated learning* if the focus changes depending on the learning intentions. For example, students may be learning how to write a procedure in a science unit on living systems. Every discipline has its own literacy. If educators can identify these literacies during the planning stage, they can integrate authentic learning opportunities.

- Reviewing work on an ongoing basis to check for understanding. Don't allow students to move on until you know they have mastered the learning. Time for reflection is imperative to assess where students are with their learning and to provide them with the chance to learn from one another, but it is often overlooked during the construction of a lesson. From the constructivist learning theory, we know students learn from processing the experience they have just had, so building it into the lesson is important.

- Providing students with the opportunity to duplicate and replicate. In our experience, duplication is uncommon in classrooms. Teachers fear that students will become disengaged, but engagement actually increases with success, which can increase in likelihood when teachers consolidate the learning by providing students the opportunity to apply their understanding in different ways.

- Encouraging memorization of critical concepts and key knowledge. This can be crucial to developing deep understanding, and it requires time. Brain research indicates that spending enough time is essential to moving information from short-term to long-term memory and ultimately achieving success in learning (Sousa, 2011). The way that teams have tackled this approach is by identifying the essential learning and subsequently allocating certain times in the week to teach them since time is limited though a process of prioritization. Many teams will also quarantine this time to ensure it is protected and free from external interruptions.

- Finding time for feedback. John Hattie (2009) indicates through his meta-analysis that feedback is essential to learning success and, out of all the strategies he investigated, was the most important factor in supporting learning. It is critical to use time to provide feedback for students in ways that connect prior and existing learning to future learning. It's not always that we don't have enough time but that we need to consider how we are using our time. The following approaches make the most of feedback in limited time.

  - Roam the room during independent practice, guided practice, and cooperative group time to observe, ask questions, monitor, and provide support.

  - Give students experiencing difficulty examples of how successful work looks.

  - Give students more than one option, asking which one they believe would be most useful to their success.

  - Provide prompts to get students started when it becomes apparent they are having difficulty.

  - Share other students' ideas, thoughts, or work plans to support the learning of their peers.

  - Give students wrong and right responses and ask them to identify and articulate which is which, and correct any student misconceptions.

- Using wait time. Providing students with time to think once the teacher has posed a question shows that we are genuinely interested in their response, and it honors the time it takes for the brain to process and respond. If the goal is a deeper level of thinking, then providing wait time is essential.

Putting the Learning in Context: Sample Scenarios

Consider the following scenarios where we outline the same learning experience in two different ways: one that is inclusive of the consideration for time and one that isn't.

Elaine's fourth-grade students are working hard on understanding the value of basic fractions, such as halves, thirds, and quarters, through pictorial representation and application. The past four weeks of the unit on fractions were designed to support students in their understanding of part numbers and their relationship to one whole, including the concept of equivalence (number values being represented differently but having the same value). Next week, the fourth-grade planner indicates that the class is moving on to teaching a unit on the introduction of decimal numbers.

Scenario One

Elaine is involved in a conference with a student, Darren, while the class is working. Darren has found it difficult to grasp the concepts taught over the previous four weeks. Elaine feels as though she hasn't really noticed the struggles Darren demonstrated in a recent summative assessment task and so wants to help him in some misconceptions he has. She feels a bit of anxiety because at the last fourth-grade meeting, the team checked the planner and agreed to move into decimals next week. It has become apparent to Elaine that Darren struggles to understand that having less than one whole means you don't have as much. In fact, the longer the conference goes on, the more aware Elaine becomes of his lack of understanding of all the knowledge and skills they have taught relating to fractions. Elaine prioritizes her response by having Darren complete a worksheet that has fractions represented as pizzas in thirds, halves, and quarters. Darren needs to shade the amount of pieces represented by the fraction amount given. She checks through the sheet with him at the end of the lesson and asks questions, hoping this has helped him understand the differences in fractional amount by both the actual number and pizza representation. The following week, Elaine introduces decimals to all the students, including Darren.

Scenario Two

Elaine is involved in a conference with a student, Darren, while the class is working. Darren has found it difficult to grasp the concepts taught over the past four weeks. Elaine, through her fourth-grade collaborative team meeting, has identified the key areas that Darren is struggling with and has provided him with time to practice some of the concepts that the team's common assessment indicated that he struggled with. She explains to Darren that she wants him to represent the fractions given as real-life amounts, such as pizza, chocolate bars, and any other whole object he can think of that might need to be broken up into parts. Darren is working alongside three others who also have similar misconceptions on the value of simple fractional amounts. She reminds him to also get help from a classroom consultant (a fourth-grade peer) who has been identified as having a strong understanding of this concept. Elaine checks a few times to clarify any questions and share observations. At the conclusion of the lesson, Elaine can see Darren and one other student still haven't got it. She lets them know that next week, during their *no-new-instruction time*, Darren will work with Miss Smith, who will ensure that he understands the concept, as both teachers and students are aware that this is an essential learning. Between now and then, Elaine plays a game with the students during lunch called *fraction lunch box*. While the students eat lunch, each student is asked to tell a fractional story that relates to what he or she is eating. For example, "I have a ham sandwich in my lunch box, but I'm only going to eat half of it because I hate ham!" The student then holds up half the sandwich.

In the second example, Elaine has carefully and deliberately considered her use of time to support the learner by:

- Providing support to Darren from another student who has demonstrated he or she understands the concept being taught
- Structuring the learning experience so that Elaine can spend time with Darren as he makes his way through the task
- Creating space in the timetable, in consultation with her colleagues, to provide additional time and support for this prioritized area of the mathematics curriculum
- Making the most of every minute by using the lunch period to make links to the key learning from the lesson to support further connections made by the students

When Consideration of Time Is Missing

When consideration of time is missing from the teacher's approach to teaching, the learning environment may show some of the following symptoms.

- Learners are moved on to the next level of instruction before fully understanding what has just been taught.
- Teachers pose questions but don't allow any time for learners to process their thinking.
- The timetable holds learning hostage and ensures an approach that is not genuinely responsive to the learning needs of students (and teachers) takes precedence.
- There is limited reflection time, including self, peer, and teacher feedback.
- Teachers may gear their lessons to the whole group as opposed to differentiating the content, process, or task based on individual needs.

- Assessments (strategies for checking for understanding) are used to find out where students are at rather than to inform their instruction and student self-assessment.
- The hit-and-hope approach to teaching takes center stage: "If I hit these learning targets through these activities, hopefully the students will get it."
- Teachers may be more likely to make decisions that are teacher centered rather than learning centered—for example, when a teacher replicates the same unit from the year before regardless of student understanding.

When Consideration of Time Is Evident

A learning culture in which time is mindfully considered may show evidence of:

- Higher levels of interaction centered on learning between students and teachers, and among students
- Higher incidents and levels of classroom-based discussion and dialogue centering on learning
- Teachers who have a deeper understanding of where their students are in their understanding of key concepts, knowledge, and skills
- More authentic approaches that cater to individual student differences, rather than generic grouping and strategies
- Teachers who are more considerate and responsive to what students say and do
- A timetable driven by the learning—not by the teaching
- More time within the timetable to flexibly respond to issues that present themselves throughout the learning experience
- A sense of calm pervading the chaos of the teaching and learning process in which wait time is a central construct

Think and Reflect

1. In what ways might you provide time to support the learning for all your students?
2. What is your sense of the way you use time that your students most value in supporting their learning?
3. Think about the times that you have learned things deeply. In what ways was time used in these situations?
4. What are some indicators for you that your conscious use of time during the learning experience is effective or ineffective in helping your students learn?

Supporting Ideas and Research

The following resources provide additional information and ideas you can use to further develop your knowledge of time.

Buffum, A., Mattos, M., & Weber, C. (2009). *Pyramid response to intervention*. Bloomington, IN: Solution Tree Press. This book explores the capacity of teams and schools to respond to students when it becomes apparent that they are in need of additional time and support. It provides practical tips on not only why we should but how we can.

Hattie, J. A. (2009). *Visible learning*. London: Routledge. John Hattie discusses the importance of time on task, emphasizing that time on task is not merely practicing a skill; it is the deliberate concentration on improving performance. He also explores the difference between mass and spaced practice.

Marzano, R. J., Pickering, D. J., & Heflebower, T. (2011). *The highly engaged classroom*. Bloomington, IN: Marzano Resources. The authors explore the concepts of pacing in lessons and the role this can play in levels of engagement for students. This includes descriptions on tasks, table work, transitions, and presenting of new content.

Rowe, M. B. (1974). Relation of wait-time and rewards to the development of language, logic, and fate control: Part II—rewards. *Journal of Research in Science Teaching*, *11*(4), 291–308. Rowe's study found that teachers wait only one second after asking a question to hear the response and even less when following up on a response. The study has been influential in reconceptualizing how we might use wait time during the teaching and learning process to elicit deeper levels of thinking in students.

Wiliam, D. (2018). *Embedded formative assessment* (2nd ed.). Bloomington, IN: Solution Tree Press. Dylan Wiliam explores and explains practical ways in which teachers can increase their capacity to use time to support understanding with students—from the way questions are organized to how time is used in responding within teacher–student and student–student interactions.

Chapter 9
Expectation

> A master can tell you what he expects of you. A teacher, though, awakens your own expectations.
>
> —Patricia Neal

Expectations are the beliefs, attitudes, and behaviors that teachers and learners project about what can be achieved. They set the standard for student achievement and paint a picture of future possibilities.

Rationale

"We have high expectations for all our students" and "We expect all our students to learn" are statements commonly heard in schools. While we agree with the sentiment in these statements, we believe that statements such as "What do high expectations look like in terms of learning?" and "What are our expectations of what the students need to understand, know, and be able to do as a result of their learning?" have far more impact. Educators will continue to lack clarity in expectations until they can collaboratively develop a common, shared understanding of student learning expectations that all teachers express to students in their individual classrooms.

This lack of clarity contributes to the discrepancy in student results. Consider the following different approaches of two high school teachers who both state what they expect all their students to achieve.

- Teacher A expects all work to be handed in if students are to receive top marks. If they don't hand in the work, students get a zero for that task and lose the chance at gaining top marks. This teacher considers her stance on tasks as evidence of having high expectations.

- Teacher B expects all work to be handed in for students to receive top marks. But if students don't hand in their work, the teacher establishes a support group during every lunchtime until the work is finished. The students receive additional support from him to work through the task and are not penalized for being late with the work.

Students who handed their work in on time have the opportunity to join this group if they believe that it would help them improve. This teacher regards this as evidence of high expectations.

So who is right? Which teacher has higher expectations? It could be argued that teacher A has higher expectations in terms of adherence to timelines but that teacher B has higher expectations of his students in terms of learning and supporting student achievement. Teachers need to be clear about expectations—what they will accept and where they will draw the line. But it's what teachers do when students are not reaching these expectations that is critical.

A number of years ago, we led a team of educators in the development of a cluster project that centered on the development of a community-based inquiry learning center called the Mornington Inquiry Learning Centre (MILC). Eight schools were involved, ranging from elementary to secondary, special to International Baccalaureate, low socioeconomic to affluent. Teachers from different schools worked together (three at a time) to plan a two-week inquiry. After planning an inquiry, teachers worked together with their students for two weeks instead of attending their regular school. At any one time, there were up to ninety students and four teachers working together for two weeks, none of whom had worked together previously. Not only did we need to develop effective ways to work, plan, and learn together, but it became apparent after the first inquiry that we needed to be very explicit about our expectations of student performance in terms of the work that they did.

What we discovered at the conclusion of the sixth inquiry was that the establishment of a high expectation for learning culture was critical to learning success. We also found that what contributed to this the most was our clarity on what we expected to see in terms of product, process, and content for students. Sharing of student work, communication of expectations, and genuine involvement of students through self-assessment against these expectations were paramount.

In a Hanover Research (2012) report prepared for the Springfield K–12 public schools district, the researchers found:

> Studies suggest that not only do students tend to increase or decrease their efforts to match the expectations laid out for them, but also that students are "reasonably accurate" in perceiving the extent to which their teachers favour some students over others by placing different expectations on them. (p. 2)

You get what you expect. So the important question becomes, What are you expecting? What helps set expectations for the students? There must be a focused and directed attention on what matters, clear and measurable benchmarks, scaffolding so that no student is left behind with an insurmountable mountain of work to climb at the end, constant feedback and recognition for excellent work, personal reflection time for students and staff, examples of high-quality work, and a culture of achievement by all. Students thrive if the expectations are high, as long as they are shown how to achieve excellence. Students want to feel pride in their work; they want to achieve. But if they are not shown how, they quickly disengage and just want to get the work done. High expectations result in high student achievement when staff are committed and persistent in setting up focused, supportive, and respectful expectations. When working with students who produce poor-quality work, teachers must first focus on how to modify their practice to support high student expectation rather than focusing on what is wrong with students. Levine and Lezotte (1990), pioneers of research on school improvement, conclude that the most effective schools in ensuring high levels of learning are those that have a climate of high expectations.

Expectation Strategies to Consider

To optimize the learning experience, teachers need to clarify their expectations, specifically when it comes to objectives for learning. What are the objectives of the learning experience for your students? What do you expect them to achieve? Notice this says *expect*, not *want*. There is a big difference between expecting students to reach desired outcomes or standards and wanting them to. The first expresses belief that they can do it, and the latter hopes that they will. As part of the objectives for learning, consider the following.

- **Key concepts:** What do you expect students to understand at a conceptual level throughout the learning experience? For example, you may expect them to know the concept of place value through the teaching of a number-based unit. You expect them to understand that the position of a number tells a story about the number's value. They have not successfully learned if they can't demonstrate this concept.

- **Key knowledge:** What do you expect students to know from the learning experience? For example, you may expect them to know that each position of a number indicates a particular value, such as ones, tens, or hundreds, or that the value of zero varies depending on its position. If they can't understand and use these key pieces of knowledge, then they have not successfully learned the concept of place value.

- **Key skill:** What do you expect students to be able to do with their newly acquired knowledge and conceptual understandings throughout the learning experience? For example, you may expect them to be able to investigate and produce a number line that represents the order of numbers they have been learning about. They can then explain to someone else how this number line helps others to understand how place value works. If they can't do this successfully, then they have not successfully learned this aspect of place value with deep understanding.

- **Key evidence:** What do you expect students to be able to do throughout the learning experience that will show you that they do understand? It may be the number line, some other key performance tasks, or another assessment task, such as a multiple-choice or short-answer test. The students are aware of what they need to demonstrate from the beginning of the unit on place value, so they can see what success would look like. The student is expected to know what a successful outcome will look like and spend his or her time working toward that. This supports the assessment for learning approach to learning success.

Putting the Learning in Context: Sample Scenarios

Consider the following scenarios that outline the same learning experience in two different ways: one that is inclusive of explicit expectations and one that is not.

Robyn has planned her class for providing feedback to her ninth-grade English literature students. This includes identifying key elements to improvement from their literature response. Each student had to write a different concluding chapter to a book of his or her choice but taken from a specified children's literature reading list.

Scenario One

The students are sitting in groups at their tables, and Robyn asks them how they felt about writing the last chapter for their chosen books. After five minutes of sharing their thoughts, Robyn reminds them that today's class is designed to support them in understanding the key elements that assist bringing high-quality children's literature together. This includes elements they have been examining all semester, including characterization, plot, setting, underlying concepts, and key author messages. Robyn hands out their assessed chapters and asks them to read through their work and her comments. She asks them to write down their reflections on what worked well and what didn't based on these key elements. After thirty minutes, she asks them to share some of their responses. She records their responses on her laptop and lets them know that she will email them the summary. She then shares the insights she made after marking their work and outlines that it is an expectation that, during their exam, they will need to consider what she shares with them. For example, the use of metaphors to highlight a key concept for the book can be a very powerful way of engaging the reader, and it was lacking in the responses she read. The students finish the class after they have noted some of her insights. She reminds them to study hard, as the exam is in a week.

Scenario Two

The students are sitting in groups at their tables. Robyn reminds them that next week's exam will assess all the learning they have been focused on during the semester. She reminds them that each week in her class the learning expectation had been clearly defined. Each was related explicitly to the elements of children's literature they were asked to include in their concluding-chapter task. She expresses her opinion that they will all succeed in the exam because of the level of commitment they have displayed to completing practice tasks each week. Supporting this belief, she hands students their chapters, including her marks and comments, to examine. She reminds them that the learning expectation for this class is to identify the key element or elements that might need focused attention between now and the exam, and to plan a strategy for deepening their understanding. She reminds them that none of the information that she provided should be a surprise to them, as they have been identifying areas of need throughout the semester and at the conclusion of each class. For example, the use of metaphors surfaced as a need during week four, and they had been given practice opportunities to apply this. As students look through their own work, Robyn conferences with them on their reflections, both individually and in groups. Toward the end of the class, she speaks to the whole group to identify areas and strategies for study between now and the exam. She shows them the connection between their ideas and the learning expectations for the unit of work that she has shared since the first lesson and every subsequent class since. She reminds them of the difference that focused attention has made to their learning so far, and she wishes them well in their study efforts.

In the second example, Robyn has demonstrated a strong use of expectations in her support of the learner by:

- Being clear about what she wanted the students to achieve and how they would do so, and then communicating it often
- Ensuring her expectations were set at the beginning of, during, and at the conclusion of the unit of work and monitored on an ongoing basis
- Communicating what she expected the students to achieve as a result of the work they had put in
- Giving the students an opportunity to practice and deepen their understandings in areas in which they were expected to demonstrate proficiency

When Expectations Are Missing

When expectations are missing from a teacher's mindful approach to teaching, the learning environment may show some of the following symptoms.

- A lack of understanding of why the learning is taking place and the relationship it has to both prior-knowledge and expected-knowledge acquisition

- Higher levels of disengagement in learning processes and tasks, both inside and outside of class
- Greater incidents of behaviors that disrupt the learning of self and others
- More time spent teaching content areas that should need less time, and less time spent teaching content areas that need more time
- Teacher dialogue that centers more on tasks rather than on the key learning that is being explored
- Assessment tasks that aren't aligned to the knowledge, skills, and dispositions being taught
- Students who express doubt about the competence and quality of the teacher, and teachers who express doubt in the competence and quality of the learner due to lessened expectations

When Expectations Are Evident

A learning culture in which expectations are mindfully considered and applied may show evidence of:

- Higher levels of student achievement linked to the opportunity for focused attention on the elements that are most critical to a learning experience
- Deeper and richer dialogue in the classroom that centers on the key concepts, knowledge, skills, and dispositions being taught
- Higher levels of accountability for learning at a variety of levels, including student-to-self, student-to-student, student-to-teacher, and teacher-to-student
- Fewer excuses for lack of learning success by both the teacher and the learner
- More explicit language used by the teacher and the learner in classroom conversations
- A greater understanding of what is needed to be successful as a learner, particularly when it relates to high-stakes assessments
- Fewer assumptions by teachers of students' progress and more success in providing strategies to support them in their individual learning needs
- Assessment tasks that support the learning of the expected outcomes

Think and Reflect

1. In what ways might you embed a culture of high expectations in your classroom?
2. What do you think your students expect to see you doing to support each of them in their learning?
3. What kinds of expectations have led you to learning things deeply?
4. What are some indicators for you that your conscious use of expectations during the learning experience are effective or ineffective in helping your students learn?

Supporting Ideas and Research

The following resources provide additional information and ideas you can use to further develop your knowledge of expectations.

Costa, A. L., & Kallick, B. (Eds.). (2008). *Learning and leading with habits of mind: 16 essential characteristics for success*. Alexandria, VA: Association for Supervision and Curriculum Development. Costa and Kallick explore the relationship between learning and having a focus on quality. This supports the ideas in this chapter on what constitutes quality and how we communicate it.

Hattie, J. A. (2009). *Visible learning*. London: Routledge. In Hattie's synthesis of more than eight hundred meta-analyses relating to student learning achievement, he articulates the power of feedback. This explicitly links to our chapter on expectations, particularly the way a teacher recognizes what students are doing well but also on what is needed in order to be successful when sharing information on what it takes.

Levine, D. U., & Lezotte, L. W. (1990). *Unusually effective schools: A review and analysis of research and practice*. Madison, WI: The National Center for Effective Schools Research and Development. The schools that are the most effective in ensuring higher levels of learning are those that have a climate of high expectations. Levine and Lezotte's longitudinal work in researching effective schools has been influential in the rationale for developing the capacity for schools to lift their level of expectation.

Marzano, R. J. (2017). *The new art and science of teaching* (Revised and expanded ed.). Bloomington, IN: Solution Tree Press. In this updated, comprehensive study and explanation of research-based instructional strategies that impact learning, Marzano outlines the role that communicating high expectations to students has on affecting teaching practice and therefore student learning. In particular, he explores how we might do this through the instructional design area of communicating high expectations.

Chapter 10
Lifeworlds

> The most important kind of freedom is to be what you really are. You trade in your reality for a role. You give up your ability to feel, and in exchange, put on a mask.
>
> —Jim Morrison

The Connecting Lives to Learning Project (Prosser, Lucas, & Reid, 2010) defines *lifeworlds* as the sites in time and space in which all of us live, referred to as our everyday life. For students, the lifeworld is not just their current reality but also their experience of their reality. It is their thoughts, feelings, and ideas about everyday life and the world in which they live.

Rationale

We first heard the term *lifeworlds* when working on the Connecting Lives to Learning Project from the research conducted by the University of South Australia. As part of that project, students were asked questions about what had helped them to learn. Their responses indicated their need (or desire) to learn as part of certain aspects of their life—for example, learning computing for work, learning to cook a certain dish for a dinner party, or learning to speak another language out of a desire to travel the world (we will speak about desire in the next chapter). The implications for schools are that if we can relate the learning to the real world of the student, we may increase the student's motivation and therefore increase success in learning.

Too often, students see learning as something that is done to them and irrelevant to their daily lives. Whether it be through the use of technology or investigating 21st century learning, educators are looking for ways to engage students. One way is to get to know students—finding out what they like, building projects around their interests—and enable them to make decisions about their learning within the context of the classroom environment.

To illustrate this point, we introduce to you Ryley, an eighth-grade student from a struggling family. While they expected him to go to school, they found it difficult to support him in his educational pursuits. He was diagnosed at least four years below grade level in both literacy and numeracy, and we discovered he had never read an entire book. He had no diagnosed learning disability, but he was bored and disinterested. He had learned how to get by in the classroom through work-avoidance strategies and misguided behavior. But he was a capable student.

He shared with us his interest in car racing and football, so we found a season highlights magazine for football, which he read to us, with us, and on his own. Throughout this process, we spoke about what good readers do (predict, use illustrations, connect to personal experience, make inferences, reread, read on, and so on). We then followed up with a short story about car racing and used the same process. By the end of the year, he had improved two grade levels on his summative assessments and was independently reading for pleasure and information in his areas of interest. It was through accessing his lifeworld that this occurred. Without that, he would have continued to disassociate himself from his schoolwork.

As teachers, we could have persevered with the class text, but to what end? How would this have helped him build his reading stamina, confidence, and appreciation? Not only had his reading capacity improved, but our relationship with him was strengthened, as it became more apparent to him that we were at least as interested in him and his world as we were in him doing the work.

As Otero, Csoti, and Rothstadt (2018) remind us, it is important to acknowledge the powerful influences of a student's life other than school and to connect learning to that knowledge and what is happening outside the school environment.

Lifeworld Connection Strategies to Consider

The following are some strategies and approaches for connecting with the students' lifeworlds. They are derived from interviews with sixty school students from both elementary and high schools that we conducted to explore what connects them to their learning.

- "Provide me with the opportunity to be the expert in the room": Most students have an interest that they are passionate about, but often teachers give only the academically capable students the opportunity to be the expert in the room. Create opportunities for students to demonstrate their skills, knowledge, and passions through carefully constructed learning experiences.
- "Discover what delights me": Often in busy classrooms, we actually forget to learn about our students, including their interests, ideas, family, and home contexts. You wouldn't plan a vacation without investigating the destination, the temperature, the culture, and the possible activities. How would you know what to pack and how to prepare and if the destination will meet your needs? Yet we often plan a unit of work or a lesson without knowing the context of our learners. We assume that, because it is in the

curriculum and we think it is interesting and relevant, our students will feel the same way. By understanding our students better, we increase the chances of engaging our students in their learning.

- "Have fun with me": Leave some time to play. Not only does this increase your knowledge of your students, but it also helps them to understand you better, forging relationships based on mutual trust and respect. Teachers and students can discover where their lifeworlds overlap, where there is common ground and difference.

- "Be interested but not intrusive": Developing an understanding of students' lifeworlds is based on respectful and supportive conversations with students, parents, teachers, and community members.

- "Give me the opportunity to make choices in my learning": Allow students to make choices that connect their learning to their lifeworld. Collaborate and construct the learning experience together, and then reflect and evaluate on its effectiveness.

- "Understand the way I communicate through technology, and provide me with resources that allow me to work effectively with technology": Today's students are digital natives. Their language is digital. Do you acknowledge and respect this in your curriculum planning and resource provision? Have conversations with students about how they think technology could better support their learning. Ask them how classrooms should look and how they could work.

Putting the Learning in Context: Sample Scenarios

Consider the following scenarios that outline the same learning experience in two different ways: one that is inclusive of the consideration of lifeworlds and one that is not.

Nathan was introducing his sixth-grade students to their upcoming unit of study—a cross-disciplinary unit on sustainable environments with focuses on both science and geography. The sixth-grade team replaced an existing unit on natural disasters with the new unit.

Scenario One

Nathan explains to the students that they will be learning about sustainable environments. He asks the students in pairs to define what they think the term *sustainable environments* means. Once students share their responses, he provides them with his working definition. The class looks for similarities. Each student is then asked in groups to draw symbols accompanied by words that highlight key features of a sustainable environment. These are to be displayed around the room to indicate what the students currently understand about the topic. At the conclusion of the lesson, students are asked to take part in a gallery walk and observe how others responded to the task.

Scenario Two

Nathan explains to the students that they will be learning about sustainable environments this term. He asks them to pair up to define what they think the term means. Once students share their responses, he provides them with his working definition. The class looks for similarities. He then asks students to identify how they feel about the topic using a scale from 1 to 10, where 1 represents *highly boring* and 10 represents *highly interesting*. He explains to his students that they must be ready to share a reason with the group for why they rated their interest as they did, physically moving to spots in the room that correlate with the numbers 1 to 10. Students' interest is spread across the scale, so he explores some of their reasons and records them on a whiteboard. Nathan then shares a story from his personal experience to assist students in understanding the concept of sustainable environments. His three-minute story outlines a time in his life when he used to go camping with his family every Easter and why he enjoyed it so much. He goes on to explain that one year his family was told they couldn't revisit that camping spot anymore because of the damage humans were doing to the area. He explained how devastated he felt as a child when he heard this news. He then asks each student in pairs to think of times when they may have been personally affected by a change in environment and to list some simple examples. He explains that the reason for doing this is to find possible lines of inquiry that they could focus on to help the whole class move from lower on the scale toward *interesting*. He provides an example of how he could use his story to come up with a line of inquiry on how to prevent human damage to natural environments. Each pair then forms groups of four and then eight to share their thinking and possibilities for inquiry. Nathan records all their ideas on the interactive whiteboard and asks them to think of those that seem most interesting to them.

In the second example, Nathan has explicitly considered the students' lifeworlds in the introduction to the unit of work. This supports the learner by:

- Providing the students with an opportunity to connect the content to personal experience or the personal experience of others (including the teacher)
- Honoring how the students feel about the learning, providing the learners with an opportunity to have input into how they can increase their interest in the content
- Providing choice on the line of inquiry they want to take through exploring connections to lifeworlds

When Connections to Lifeworlds Are Missing

When lifeworlds are missing from a teacher's mindful approach to teaching, the learning environment may show some of the following symptoms.

- A lack of interest on the part of the learner, who is more engaged through compliance and fear of consequence than interest in learning
- Students who don't connect what they are learning to their lives
- Teachers who may be perceived by some students as not caring about them or their specific concerns and learning needs
- Students who may perceive teachers as not understanding them or at the very least not trying to understand them
- A classroom culture in which learning is done to the students rather than done with the students
- A lack of mutual respect, leading to poor-quality and compromised learning relationships
- Higher incidents of both overt and covert misbehavior
- A greater proportion of students asking, "Why are we doing this?"

When Connections to Lifeworlds Are Evident

A learning culture in which lifeworlds are mindfully considered and applied may show evidence of:

- Student voices expressed through the learning experience
- Learners who are able to connect their personal experiences more readily to the learning at hand
- A mutual respect between the teacher and learner
- A greater proportion of students on task and generally interested in the learning
- More inquiry-based approaches to learning taking place
- Higher levels of student achievement and attendance
- A healthy respect between teacher and learner, with fewer assumptions made and more facts sought
- A more personalized approach to learning demonstrated through dialogue between teacher and students (for example, "I know this is not something you find easy, but I'd like you to think about it in this way")

Think and Reflect

1. In what ways may you develop an understanding of your students' lifeworlds?
2. How might this understanding influence your planning?
3. In what ways do you have fun with your students?
4. In what ways do you encourage your students to exhibit their expertise and passions within the classroom context?
5. In what ways might you encourage the use of technology within your classroom to be more inclusive of the digital native?
6. In what ways might you provide students with the opportunity to collaboratively construct their learning experience?

Supporting Ideas and Research

The following resources provide additional information and ideas you can use to further develop your knowledge of lifeworlds.

Ellum, L., & Longmuir, F. (2013). *A different journey*. Melbourne, Australia: Bayside and Glen Eira Kingston Local Learning and Employment Network. In this publication is a key finding on the research of what children who are at educational risk need, including flexible approaches to learning, strong relationships, and links to a real context.

Jacobs, H. H. (Ed.). (2010). *Curriculum 21: Essential education for a changing world*. Alexandria, VA: Association for Supervision and Curriculum Development. Chapter 12, "Creating Learning Connections With Today's Tech-Savvy Student" by Bill Sheskey, provides an interesting view on the role of technology in the 21st century classroom.

Marzano, R. J. (1992). *A different kind of classroom*. Alexandria, VA: Association for Supervision and Curriculum Development. In this text, Marzano explores how we ask students to use the knowledge that they acquire. He provides strategies that will encourage students to apply knowledge in meaningful ways that link to their personal interests.

Prosser, B., Lucas, W., & Reid, A. (2010). *Connecting lives and learning: Renewing pedagogy in the middle years*. Cambridge, MA: Wakefield Press. This book provides research and case studies supporting the idea that, through connecting lifeworlds to learning, huge inroads can be made to increasing both student engagement and achievement.

Otero, G., Csoti, R., & Rothstadt, D. (2018). *Creating powerful learning relationships: A whole-school community approach* (2nd ed.). Melbourne, Australia: Hawker Brownlow Education. This text stresses the importance of acknowledging the powerful influences of the student's life other than school, and the need for us to connect learning to what is happening outside the school environment.

Chapter 11
Desire

It is the supreme art of the teacher to awaken joy in creative expression and knowledge.

—Albert Einstein

Desire is a strong wanting or a wishing for something. It is the urge that drives our motivation to engage in things. Desire precedes purpose and ambition. Without desire, we have no urgency to work toward a goal, as desire is the fuel that ignites our action.

Rationale

Desire is closely linked to motivation and interest. Desire is fueled by motivation and interest and vice versa. When we have a desire to learn something, we are more naturally interested and motivated to learn it, although desire can also build over time. Sousa and Tomlinson (2018) surmise key neuroscience findings in this field when they state, "High motivation leads to greater attention, curiosity, and increased willingness to learn. . . . High motivation leads to greater interest, and high interest is intrinsically motivating" (p. 126). One might infer that it's important, therefore, that teachers as architects of learning construct approaches that build both from and toward a desire to learn.

Think about the last time you learned about something. What were the reasons for learning it? Was it need, interest, passion, or because you were told you had to? We will examine these whys in a personal example.

Recently, I (Gavin) bought a Mac after using a PC for the last twenty years. Why would I put myself and my family through the stress of this? Because I believe the programs and quality for photos and videos are better. Why is this important to my decision? Because I like to make movies of the family each year, incorporating photos and videos to capture what we did—for now and posterity.

Why is this important to me? Because I believe my kids benefit socially and emotionally through viewing the things they have experienced over the years. I also believe they would find the videos extremely satisfying in the event that something was to happen to me, my wife, or both of us. Because I believe it supports the building of identity for my kids, both independently and interdependently (as part of the family). Because I love my kids and want what I perceive is best for them.

On the outside, it may have seemed that I bought the Mac for its software and aesthetic reasons. But the bottom line is that it was about my children. This desire fueled my decision to dispense with what I had always known (a PC world) and to embark on a new technological journey. Now, I had the freedom to make this choice, but in schools we are not necessarily so fortunate. We have to teach certain concepts, knowledge, and skills. Not all of those will naturally meet the desire of our students to learn it. I know I wasn't exactly over the moon about learning algebra, but some other students were.

Csikszentmihalyi (1997), in *Finding Flow: The Psychology of Engagement With Everyday Life*, proposes that when we are really engaged in what we are doing, we enter a state of *flow*, when time stands still and we are truly focused on what we are doing. This state of flow is strongly linked to desire. If you have the opportunity to watch children play, you will notice how quickly and easily they get into a state of flow.

The key for teachers is to be able to generate an interest in the content they are required to teach. This requires careful consideration when planning learning experiences. We recognize not all students are interested, and that becomes patently clear when we see the ways they behave. Our experience has been that the older students get, the less automatic their interests and engagement become. Therefore, teachers need to be more strategic when working with them. So how can we generate this desire for learning?

Desire-Generating Strategies to Consider

Teachers can utilize a variety of strategies to spark curiosity in students and their desire to apply themselves. The following strategies and approaches are just some for generating desire and come from the study by Prosser, Lucas, and Reid (2010). Approaches to create challenging learning tasks that fuel desire include the following.

- **Planning teaching and learning sequences:** Making sure students can see clearly the sequence of learning means they are more likely to be able to make connections to past and future learning.
- **Having students produce significant outcomes or products:** When students are able to see a tangible use for the outcomes of their learning or product, they may be more likely to be motivated to learn about it.

- **Building negotiation in at various stages:** Student ownership and choice can build a desire to learn, as the students feel part of the learning process.
- **Explicitly emphasizing what is most important:** Highlighting for students what is most critical and worthy of more effort assists them to feel potentially less overwhelmed and positive in their belief that they can achieve it.

Approaches for developing strong connectedness to fuel desire in learning include:

- Generating themes that come from student and community concerns so that the students see the relevance of what they are learning to the real world
- Building classrooms that function as research centers so that the students genuinely contribute to the building of knowledge
- Involving students in producing their own knowledge to assist them in generating greater interest in what they are learning about
- Using integrated approaches to learning with topics of student interest, such as:
  - Diet and fast food
  - Student lifeworld issues that need resolving, like conflict
  - Biographies of family members
  - Popular culture
  - Interviews with an expert in a high-interest area
  - Science in the local environment
  - Youth culture identity research and presentation
  - Photo-story literacy work based on personal or cultural stories
  - Problem-solving issues in the local area
  - Local or school groups and legal studies
  - Histories of local buildings
  - Class newspapers that cover a variety of issues

Finding an Authentic Audience for Student Learning

The term *authentic* in this context refers to forms or demonstrations of student learning achievements to audiences wider than the teacher and other students in the class. These can include exhibitions, multimedia presentations, and artifacts to be shown to a wider audience. This might include things such as magazines, presentations to panels, or group performances. These approaches are a natural way of integrating information and communication technology into the learning experience. For example, students can create:

- Claymation films in art class
- Podcasts in science
- PowerPoint presentations in mathematics

- Models in mathematics or the humanities
- Oral presentations that are filmed
- Student-led conferences
- Roundtable exhibitions
- Digital or paper portfolios
- Articles in newsletters
- YouTube video projects

Create a playful learning environment. Often the greatest scientific discoveries have been made unintentionally. The discovery of antibiotics is one example. The process of playing with knowledge, concepts, and materials allows for such discovery. It enables the individual to have fun and manipulate and examine previous understandings to build new understandings. Providing students with the opportunity to play with understandings and skills is highly motivating, as it increases their internal desire to learn by giving them control of the learning process.

You can encourage playful learning environments by:

- Encouraging students to try, and to not be afraid to make errors, by communicating how important it is to the learning process on a regular basis and when needed
- Providing students with unstructured time to play with new information and technology as opposed to just giving them free time, and building play into the class schedule so that a culture of playfulness develops
- Developing a *new ideas* and an *I wonder* graffiti board in the classroom
- Having plenty of creative and concrete materials that students can access to support their thinking
- Actively teaching creativity
- Teaching concepts through playful games
- Modeling playfulness
- Using technology in playful ways (for example, many apps provide students with the opportunity to play with a concept in a very engaging forum)

By clarifying expectations around what students are learning, providing challenging learning tasks, connecting the learning so it is relevant, enabling students to authentically apply the learning, and creating playful learning environments, teachers can increase students' level of desire to engage in the learning itself.

Putting the Learning in Context: Sample Scenarios

Increasing students' desire to learn is a critical consideration when engaging learners in the learning experience. Consider the following scenarios that outline the same learning experience in two different ways: one that is inclusive of the consideration of desire and one that is not.

John is an eleventh-grade English teacher passionate about his subject. He has the task of supporting his students to understand key concepts explored in the novel *Animal Farm.*

Scenario One

John asks his eleventh-grade class to read *Animal Farm* by George Orwell over the school's break. After the break, he discusses with his class the main contentions in the book and provides students with a handout of notes he has taken as a way of supporting those students who either haven't read the book or are not clear about the main contentions. He writes an essay topic on the board and puts the students in small groups to discuss their writing ideas as a way of supporting those who are not really motivated. He notices that the level of conversation in the groups is limited and usually dominated by one or two people. He also notices quite a bit of disruptive behavior in the groups.

Scenario Two

John introduces the topic of power and control to his eleventh-grade English students. He explains that after the break, they are going to use the text *Animal Farm* by George Orwell to help explore the concept. He provides them with a writing continuum of skills that they are going to master through exploring the text. He asks them to identify the writing skills that they are already competent in and also those that they would like to focus on through exploring the text. The skills the students have identified are then written up as learning goals, and he discusses with individual students what they hope to achieve (their learning goals) and makes suggestions as to how they could work toward these goals. He then groups students by shared learning goals for his explicit teaching groups.

To engage his students in the topic, he asks them to individually reflect on the following question: Who controls my life?

He uses the following prompts to support student thinking: Are you free to do whatever you please? If not, why not? Do you think this is fair? What could you do about it if you wanted this to change? Can you do anything? If you could, why haven't you yet?

He asks the students to think about a time when they were not allowed to do something they wanted to do. What happened? Was it fair? How did they feel as a consequence? What happened next?

After individual reflections, he asks the students to share their narratives in small groups. He asks each group to identify any common themes in the discussions and how they relate to power. He also asks the groups to identify anything that they feel needs to be changed (for example, wearing a school uniform). The groups give feedback to the class, and as a class, students identify common themes and link them back to the concepts of power and control.

John then explains that *Animal Farm* is about what they had been discussing and provides an example about people wanting to have more control over their lives. He tempts his students by saying that it would be interesting to see whether they agreed with the way the characters went about getting change and whether they felt it was successful.

At this stage, John asks the students to read *Animal Farm* and lets them know that he has also provided an audio version, uploaded onto the school website, for students who may choose to experience the text in this way.

In the second example, John has carefully and deliberately increased his students' desire to engage in the learning in a number of ways by:

- Supporting them to set their own learning goals, focusing on their current skill level
- Discussing a learning plan with students to support them in reaching their goals
- Connecting their own life experiences to the main concepts
- Providing opportunities for them to play with their understandings before engaging with the text

When Desire Is Missing

When student desire is missing, the learning environment may show the following symptoms.

- **Students unable to start tasks:** Procrastination may be an indication that a student's desire to engage in the topic is low and, more importantly, that the student is not engaged in the learning process.
- **Challenging behavior:** Disengagement begins to develop as a result of a

low desire to engage in the learning. Challenging behavior is not just external behaviors but also internalized behaviors, such as withdrawal and avoidance. If you have students who exhibit externalizing and internalizing behaviors, it is worth investigating how motivated they are to learn and what strategies you could use to increase their motivation.

- **Noncompletion of tasks:** If students are not hooked into the learning, task completion will be challenging, especially with tasks that require sustained application.

- **Low achievement levels and poor learning growth:** This can be a result of the previous three symptoms. Students who are not active in their own learning don't learn. Teachers can create a seemingly wonderful learning experience for students, but if they have no desire to engage in the learning, it serves no purpose.

- **Teacher frustration:** Teachers might feel like they aren't getting through to some students who are not responding to the learning. If students do not want to engage in the learning experiences, motivation and desire could be the barrier.

When Desire Is Evident

When students have a desire to learn and engage in the learning process, you will see:

- Students who are clear on what they are learning and why
- High student engagement, leading to task completion
- Knowledge generation and innovation
- Positive interactions between students, and between students and the teacher
- Students talking about the topic that is either planned or unexpected
- Students wanting to discuss their learning and show you what they are doing
- Students self-regulating and self-assessing
- Students actively making decisions about their learning
- Learning growth and high levels of learning achievement
- Learning outcomes of which students are proud
- High levels of positive emotions
- Playfulness and humor within the classroom
- Good attendance levels

Think and Reflect

1. How might you foster in your students a desire to learn?

2. How might you respond when students are not motivated to learn?

3. What opportunities might you provide that allow your students to express what it is that they desire to learn?

4. How might you respond to their desires?

5. What could you do to monitor your own levels of motivation and how this transfers into the learning experience?

6. How might you measure your students' desire to learn?

7. How do you make the learning intentions explicit?

8. How might you enable students to assess their own level of competence and set learning goals?

9. How do you ensure that your students are challenged?

10. How might you increase playfulness in your classroom culture?

11. What authentic opportunities do you provide for students to do something with what they have learned?

Supporting Ideas and Research

The following resources provide additional information and ideas you can use to further develop your knowledge of desire.

Bransford, J. D., Brown, A. L., & Cocking, R. R. (2000). *How people learn: Brain, mind, experience, and school* (Expanded ed.). Washington, DC: National Academies Press. This text provides an interesting breakdown of the elements of motivation in learning, with a particular focus on the perceived usefulness of the learning.

Costa, A. L., & Kallick, B. (Eds.). (2008). *Learning and leading with habits of mind: 16 essential characteristics for success*. Alexandria, VA: Association for Supervision and Curriculum Development. This resource offers many useful examples of strategies and concepts to increase students' motivation to learn and develop students' awareness of their own learning habits.

Csikszentmihalyi, M. (1997). *Finding flow: The psychology of engagement with everyday life*. New York: Basic Books. This text provides an in-depth insight into the concept of flow, which is strongly linked to engagement and motivation.

Hattie, J. (2009). *Visible learning*. London: Routledge. This text provides evidence of the importance of creating a playful environment in which error is encouraged and, in addition, the importance of recognizing that motivation is not solely talking about engaging with the content topic but, more importantly, engaging with the learning process.

Jacobs, H. H. (Ed.). (2010). *Curriculum 21: Essential education for a changing world*. Alexandria, VA: Association for Supervision and Curriculum Development. In chapter 12, discussion centers on the power of technology in increasing students' desire to learn.

Marzano, R. J. (1992). *A different kind of classroom*. Alexandria, VA: Association for Supervision and Curriculum Development. In this resource, Robert Marzano explores how we ask students to use the knowledge they acquire. He provides strategies that will encourage students to use knowledge meaningfully and emphasizes the need to let the student hold the locus of control in the learning process.

Otero, G., Csoti, R., & Rothstadt, D. (2018). *Creating powerful learning relationships: A whole-school community approach* (2nd ed.). Melbourne, Australia: Hawker Brownlow Education. This text stresses the importance of acknowledging the powerful influences of the student's life other than school and the need for us to connect learning to what is happening outside the school environment.

Schrage, M. (2000). *Serious play: How the world's best companies simulate to innovate.* Boston: Harvard Business School Press. Even though this book primarily focuses on stimulating innovation in the workplace, it has many implications for the ways in which we structure the learning environment in schools and in particular how we grow creativity.

Seligman, M. E. P. (2011). *Flourish*. New York: Free Press. This text helps us to examine motivation as a key contributor to well-being and provides some useful concepts and strategies on increasing motivation.

Tomlinson, C. A. (2003). *Fulfilling the promise of the differentiated classroom*. Alexandria, VA: Association for Supervision and Curriculum Development. This and many of Tomlinson's other books provide classroom strategies to ensure students are engaged through challenging learning tasks.

Chapter 12
Resources

> You cannot afford to wait for perfect conditions. Goal setting is often a matter of balancing timing against available resources. Opportunities are easily lost while waiting for perfect conditions.
>
> —Gary Ryan Blair

Resources are the human and nonhuman skills and materials that support the learning process. Carefully selected, designed, and used, they are an integral part of the learning process and can aid in scaffolding understanding.

Rationale

Human and nonhuman resources make the business of learning easier, but it is imperative to ensure that the right resources are used at the right time. Marzano (2017) identifies his thirteenth element to the art and science of teaching as providing resources and guidance for students. He identifies books, websites, videos, diagrams, and material resources, such as models or building materials, as important in the provision of resources that ask students to apply knowledge they have learned.

To highlight the importance of resources, I (Clare) will share a personal anecdote. My son is a cooking fanatic (unfortunately not so passionate about cleaning up). Somehow, in the hectic family schedule, he converted us all into following the cooking reality-television show *MasterChef*. Weekly we were astounded by the cooking feats that the amateur chef competitors created, and we all became highly motivated to raise the bar of expectations for our own common dinner menu. So renewed was our cooking confidence that, as a family, we lightly took on the challenge to create our own croquembouche for an important family function, boldly making the statement that a celebration cake need not be ordered from the traditional pastry chef—we would provide it. We all felt assured in our ability to do so; after all, we had watched exemplars model the process, we all had the desire, and we all had a reasonable amount of cooking skill, as well as step-by-step instructions printed off the *MasterChef* website—how hard could it be?

We bought what we thought were the right ingredients, if not exactly the same as those on the recipe sheet, and set aside a whole day to construct our croquembouche. What we discovered as we went through the process was that (1) we didn't have the right equipment or some of the right ingredients and (2) we needed at least one human resource (cooking expert) standing beside us. The results were disastrous. We turned up to the family function carrying a plate holding what looked like a spaceship soaked in maple syrup. We were deflated and embarrassed. My son and I later attended a workshop in a professional kitchen that taught us how to make a croquembouche. Having the right equipment and an exemplar human resource (the teacher) made all the difference, and we can both attest to knowing how to make a croquembouche now.

When we reflect on our experiences with our families and how these experiences might transfer into some of our observations within the school environment, we can see many parallels. How often do carefully constructed learning experiences end in frustrations because of either a lack of the right resources or simply a lack of resources?

An example of this is one we are sure most teachers have experienced: when a well-designed information-and-communications-technology (ICT) learning experience falls apart because of glitches or lack of computers. The skill of the architect designing the learning experience must lie in the ability to match the planned learning experience with carefully tailored learning resources. An architect planning a building must take into consideration the building materials available and their suitability for the design. As teachers, we must also be mindful of this as we design the learning experience, asking ourselves, "What resources are available, and how suitable are they for what is planned?"

Resource Strategies to Consider

Write a list of all the possible resources that would support your planned learning experience. Revisit the list and check that the possible resources align directly with the desired learning outcome and are not simply related fillers. The resources should facilitate the learner developing a deeper understanding of the desired learning by the following.

- **Assisting with generating understanding:** Interactive and noninteractive resources can greatly assist learners by catering to multiple learning approaches. Some examples include DVDs, computer-based games, guest speakers, ICT, manipulative aides and resources, incursions and excursions, iPads, interactive web platforms, CDs, reading materials, digicams, cameras, and so on.

- **Focusing attention:** Resources can help students focus attention on what they are learning. The important consideration is not simply to use a resource because it is great but rather to use a resource because it will assist students in focusing their learning. The critical question when using a resource is whether or not the resource is assisting the learner to focus or distracting the learner from the learning.

- **Scaffolding the learning experience:** Effective resources play a role in scaffolding the learning experience by effectively moving the student from a sensory experience to cognitive perception and, finally, to understanding. An example of this is the use of base-ten blocks when introducing the concept of counting on. The base-ten blocks provide the learner with a sensory experience of counting on, scaffolding the learning experience, which in time will allow him or her to create an internal representation of what counting on actually is. Resources can assist moving the learner from a sensory experience to an internal representation. Critical to success is how teachers skilfully use resources within a learning experience to assist understanding.

- **Providing the opportunity for practice and consolidation:** Effective resources provide students with the opportunity to practice and consolidate what they are learning in a fun and interactive way. This could be through the use of cognitive tools, multimedia, interactive games, worksheets, manipulative tools, or technology. Using different resources for practicing allows students to navigate their own learning in terms of what works for them.

- **Encouraging the performance of learning:** Students can demonstrate their learning in a plethora of ways given the opportunity and a variety of resources. They can make documentaries, construct models, record music, run radio and web-based forums, design websites, produce films, create artwork, compile digital portfolios, or write and present stories. Providing quality resources that support students as they perform their learning sends a strong message that teachers place a high value on their learning.

Putting the Learning in Context: Sample Scenarios

Consider the following scenarios where we outline the same learning experience in two different ways: one that is inclusive of resources and one that isn't.

Jackie is an early-elementary educator who has been teaching for two years. She has a lively prep class, and she wants to explore the outcome that centers on students being effective communicators. More explicitly, the outcome states students express ideas and make meaning using a range of media. For example, "Use language and engage in play to imagine and create roles, scripts, and ideas."

Scenario One

Jackie decides that she is going to encourage the students to retell their play stories at the end of the session to support them in developing their communication skills. She sets up the tables with a range of resources and discusses what she is hoping the students will do at the end of the session before they begin their play. During the play session, a number of arguments break out over some of the toys that are in high demand, and she notices that there are some toys that the students are not playing with. To manage the arguments, Jackie directs students to the toys that are available to avoid any further conflict. At the end of the session, the two learning support staff clean up while Jackie sits with the students and asks them to share their play stories individually. She feels a little frustrated, as after the first four sharings, the students get restless and start wriggling around. She also is not sure how to manage the students who share in such detail and are taking up too much time.

Scenario Two

Jackie decides that she is going to encourage the students to retell their play stories at different times throughout the session to support them in developing their communication skills. Over the past few weeks, Jackie and the learning support staff have been observing which toys have high play value for the students. Instead of setting up the tables with activities, Jackie shows the students visual pictures and film clips of some play scenarios and retells the play story as a way of modeling to the students but also to give them some play ideas. Jackie and her staff have organized the room so that the students can individually choose what they want to play with from a range of toys and materials on display. The tables are not set up prior to the sessions, but there are areas around the room that have been carefully arranged to encourage play themes. Jackie explains to the students that she and her helpers (including parents whom she has briefed) will be coming around to chat about their play and taking photos for their learning journals. As the session progresses, Jackie and the helpers get the opportunity to chat to individual students and encourage them to share their play story. Often this turns into a collaborative effort with other students joining in. Before the end of the session, Jackie stops the students and lets them know it is pack-up time. The students are responsible for packing their toys up. While this is happening, the helpers print the photos and glue them into the learning journals. The students take home their learning journals to show their parents and caregivers and tell their play stories. The parents and caregivers are provided with information before this happens and encouraged to write their own comments on the page as a response to their children's play stories.

In the second example, Jackie has mindfully considered her use of resources to support the learner by:

- Planning the resources that will be used in advance and what they will be used for explicitly
- Organizing the resources into designated areas within the classroom that serve a purpose for the lesson
- Integrating digital technology resources (cameras) into the learning experience and utilizing them for the purpose of self-reflection and building the learning partnership between school and the home
- Utilizing the resources to support discovery learning within a structure as opposed to just putting resources out on tables for free play

When Resources Are Missing

When resources, both human and nonhuman, are not key constructs within the learning environment, the following symptoms may be evident.

- Lack of connection to the work. Both human and nonhuman resources enable learners to make powerful connections between concrete and abstract concepts. When resources are poorly matched to the learning task, learners may be unable to connect to the work and make the powerful links from concrete experiences to abstract and complex concepts. Take, for example, self-assessment. If learners are not supported in developing skills of self-assessment through modeling (human resource) and are not provided with adequate assessment tools such as continuums, rubrics, and exemplars (nonhuman), they are unlikely to connect to the processes required for self-assessment.
- Challenging behavior and poor motivation. Learning environments that are not well resourced to support independent learning may, in fact, promote challenging behavior. Learners unable to seek out resources to problem-solve and work independently may express their frustration through their behavior. It is hard to build a house without the right tools; likewise, it is hard to learn without the right tools.
- A chaotic learning environment. Imagine a building site with many different tools and tradespeople all eager to work together to start the build. Imagine further that on one particular day, well into the building project, some tradespeople didn't turn up and some of those who did turn up forgot their tools. To keep the building project going, the present tradespeople tried to do the jobs of those who were missing without the skills and by making do with the tools they had. What would happen? Chaos! It is no different in a learning environment that is poorly resourced. Most learners will try to make do, but the learning environment will feel chaotic and unpredictable. High levels of learner anxiety may be an indicator of a chaotic learning environment.

- Poor transference. Well-designed resources enable learners to achieve deep levels of transference and generative knowledge. Lack of resources may result in superficial learning in which the learner has no real understanding and cannot transfer the learning in a new or different context.

- Teacher stress. If the teacher's stress levels within the classroom are high, it may be a result of poorly managed or inadequate resources. If the learning environment is not stocked with adequate resources, learners will struggle with working independently and, as a consequence, will be much more demanding on teacher time. The greatest resource within the learning environment is the learner and his or her ability to regulate his or her own learning, but to do so, the learner needs the right tools and for the tools to be accessible in an orderly environment.

- Poor quality and quantity output because learners lack the resources to create products or they haven't learned the knowledge.

- Task failure due to a lack of support in assisting students to make connections, utilize models, or represent learning in different ways, or due to one-dimensional support.

When Resources Are Evident

When resources are well thought out and well used, you will see:

- High learning engagement: Learners who are well supported through adequate resourcing will feel confident and capable of achieving their learning goals.

- High levels of learning transference: Resources that are well matched to the learning task enable learners to make powerful connections between concrete and abstract concepts.

- High-quality task completion and learning: Going back to our building site example, if builders have the right tools and the right level of human resources, they can use their knowledge and skills to build a great house. It is no different for learners within the learning environment. Given the right tools and support, they can use their current understandings, knowledge, and skills to build new understandings, skills, and knowledge, resulting in high-quality task completion and learning.

- High levels of independent learning: Learners who feel confident using the resources teachers provide are able to monitor their own learning and work independently. Well-designed resources enable learners to tap into their inner resources and develop confidence in their own abilities to solve problems. This includes the skills of identifying and articulating what resources students feel they need to support their learning.

- An orderly and inviting classroom culture: If learners feel that the resources they have access to enable them to learn effectively, they will value those resources. This will be evident in how students care for the resources and take pride in the learning environment. The learning environment should be well organized so that learners know where and how to find resources to support their learning.

- Low levels of teacher and learner anxiety: When the learning environment supports the learner with appropriate resources, teacher and learner stress is well managed, and anxiety levels remain low. Chaotic, stressful learning environments may result in cortisol, a powerful neurotransmitter, being released in the brain. Cortisol works against learners being able to focus and attend by putting the brain in flight-or-fight mode. By reducing learner and teacher stress levels through the provision of well-designed resources, teachers contribute to reducing the risk of learning anxiety and the resultant cortisol release.

Think and Reflect

1. How might you align resources with the understandings, knowledge, and skills you wish to develop in your students?
2. How could you use resources to generate understandings?
3. How might you use resources to assist students to develop focused attention?
4. How might you use resources to scaffold learning?
5. How might you use resources to provide opportunities to practice and consolidate learning?
6. How could you use resources to support students to articulate their learning?

Supporting Ideas and Research

The following resources provide additional information and ideas you can use to further develop your knowledge of resources.

Costa, A. L., & Kallick, B. (Eds.). (2008). *Learning and leading with habits of mind: 16 essential characteristics for success.* Alexandria, VA: Association for Supervision and Curriculum Development. In the section that deals with thinking independently, Costa and Kallick explore the use of visual tools to support learning.

Danielson, C. (2007). *Enhancing professional practice: A framework for teaching* (2nd ed.). Alexandria, VA: Association for Supervision and Curriculum Development. In Domain 2: the classroom environment, Carol Danielson outlines how effective teachers may manage resources to support higher levels of learning.

Jacobs, H. H. (Ed.). (2010). *Curriculum 21: Essential education for a changing world.* Alexandria, VA: Association for Supervision and Curriculum Development. In chapter 12, "Creating Learning Connections With Today's Tech-Savvy Student," Bill Shesky discusses at length the opportunities that arise from using technology within the classroom. He questions why we ban students' portable devices when they could be powerful learning tools.

Marzano, R. (1992). *A different kind of classroom.* Alexandria, VA: Association for Supervision and Curriculum Development. The discussion centers on the utility of graphic organizers within the learning framework.

Prosser, B., Lucas, W., & Reid, A. (2010). *Connecting lives and learning.* Cambridge, MA: Wakefield Press. This book provides research and case studies on managing students in learning. Many cases are made for community-based, school, classroom, and human resources alongside ICT resources being integral to the learning needs of students.

Chapter 13
Existing Knowledge

> Education is the kindling of a flame, not the filling of a vessel.
>
> —Socrates

Existing knowledge is the unique bank of stored understandings an individual has built over his or her lifetime. It is shaped through experience and stored consciously and unconsciously in long-term memory. Existing knowledge, once activated, serves to assist the learner to make crucial links between old and new information and therefore assists with developing new understandings.

Rationale

By the time students enter the formal learning environment of school, they have had millions of experiences and interactions. They have developed understandings that are continually being strengthened, modified, and even replaced. They have developed neurological pathways encoded by their experiences. As they continue to develop, their experiences continue to shape the architecture of their brains. As creators of the learning experience, we must be mindful of how we influence students' understanding of the world around them. We need to design learning experiences that are efficient in terms of processing, storing, and retrieving information. To do this, we must explore what students already know so that we can build on, refine, modify, and even eradicate it if it is built on false assumptions.

To design a learning experience efficiently, we need to base it on students' existing knowledge. One of the things that we have tried to do throughout this book is use examples of life experiences that we can all relate to. Teachers should explore three questions as they plan the learning experience.

1. How will I determine what my students already know?
2. How will this influence the designed learning experience?
3. How can I effectively build on my students' existing knowledge?

Existing knowledge can be a barrier to learning success, as we know through children who struggle to learn how to read in the early years of schooling. Because of a lack of phonological awareness, phonemic awareness, vocabulary development, alphabetic principles, and print knowledge in early childhood, students can be at a disadvantage before they even begin.

But as Campbell and Campbell (2009) point out:

> It would be a mistake to think that prior knowledge's only influence on learning is negative. This is not the case. Learning ultimately begins with the known and proceeds to the unknown. Connecting everyday experiences with classroom topics and intentionally engaging preexisting knowledge with new classroom content can promote meaningful and lasting learning. (p. 11)

Strategies to Consider for Determining Existing Knowledge

Develop a range of tools that will assist in formatively assessing students' existing knowledge, such as:

- A variety of thinking tools to ascertain what students already know (for example, lotus charts, concept maps, fish bones, graffiti boards, affinity diagrams, brainstorms, and KWL [know, want to know, learned] charts)
- A variety of discussion tools to generate conversation around a topic (for example, round-robin, think-pair-share, five questions, true/false lists, and ranking lists)
- Opportunities for informal conversations and student feedback to determine how well matched the learning is to students' current knowledge
- Introducing a unit of work by integrating the knowledge of experts in the room into the learning experience while providing opportunities for the experts to continue to deepen their understandings
- Using rubrics that allow students to formatively assess their own existing knowledge
- Developing continuums around essential learnings that are student friendly and displayed for students to formatively assess where they are on a continuum

Encourage students to develop skills in linking new information to existing knowledge by:

- **Providing opportunities for learning through social thinking:** Model through thinking out loud and linking existing information to new information. Vygotsky, Hanfmann, and Vakar (2012) state students learn to think by listening to others think out loud.
- **Explicitly pointing out any links to prior knowledge:** Revisit previous relevant learning as a way of introducing new learning. For example, say, "I would like you to share with your partner what we learned in mathematics yesterday and between you come up with three things that you learned. . . . Today we are going to build on that learning by…"

- **Using questioning as a way of prompting students to think how information might relate to existing knowledge:** For example, say, "Can anyone think how what we have just discussed might relate to what we spoke about last term in . . . ?"

Putting the Learning in Context: Sample Scenarios

Consider the following scenarios that outline the same learning experience in two different ways: one that is inclusive of the consideration of existing knowledge and one that is not.

Blair is teaching a lesson to his twelfth-grade legal studies students. The focus for this class is on arresting powers and legislation. He has a set curriculum and specific points to teach, which have been provided for him as a PowerPoint. These include referring to readings from the set textbook. The lesson is to last for an hour.

Scenario One

The students take their seats in the classroom. Blair introduces them to what they will be covering for the hour and shares some key principles of the history and rationale for legislation on arresting powers in their state. His slide refers students to page 121 of their textbook and asks them to read the five paragraphs on that page. Once he has provided them with this time, he talks about what the key points of that reading are and directs them to the questions on page 122 to answer. He individually helps students as they work through the questions and stops them halfway through to share some pictures of different situations where an arrest is or is not about to take place. He asks them to match the picture on screen with the scenarios they just read about on page 121. He continues to answer clarifying questions and, as the hour draws to an end, asks for any general questions from the class. He finishes with key points from the PowerPoint to summarize the areas most important for students to remember when it comes to exam time. The students take notes and write down references for study, and the class is finished.

Scenario Two

The students take their seats in the classroom. Blair introduces them to what they will be covering for the hour and shares some key principles of the history and rationale for legislation of arresting powers in their state. His slide refers students to page 121 of their textbook, and he asks them to read the five paragraphs on that page. But before he asks them to do this, he organizes the students into trios. He asks them to brainstorm a response to the following question: In terms of arresting powers and legislation, what information do you already know in this area of our topic?

He scaffolds the discussion and asks each member of the trio to talk uninterrupted for two minutes. If they can't think of anything to say, the group is instructed just to pause. Blair times each round of two minutes. Once the three rounds are completed, he asks each trio to brainstorm their initial responses for five minutes. At the end of this time, he collates and records the key information from the group.

Blair then links what they already know to the text on page 121. He suggests that they spend their time reading just paragraphs three, four, and five because they have a good handle on the first two paragraphs. He then asks them to answer only those corresponding questions on page 122. He individually helps students as they work through the questions and stops them halfway through to show some pictures of different situations where an arrest is or is not about to take place. He asks them to match the pictures on the screen with the scenarios that they have just read about on page 121 and the discussions they had about their prior knowledge. He continues to answer clarifying questions and, as the hour draws to an end, asks for any general questions. He finishes with key points from the PowerPoint to summarize which areas are most important for them to focus on when it comes to exam time. The students take notes and write down references for study, and the class is finished.

In the second example, Blair has carefully and deliberately considered the prior knowledge students bring to the learning by:

- Planning a specific question that relates to background knowledge students might have that is related to the topic
- Adjusting tasks based on what the students fed back to him and remaining flexible in his teaching approach based on what he heard
- Extrapolating the most important information the students need to focus on in the future based on the knowledge that they have demonstrated they already have
- Using the textbook as a support to their existing knowledge

When Consideration of Existing Knowledge Is Missing

When accessing prior knowledge is not a key consideration within the learning environment, the following symptoms may be evident.

- Teachers may implicitly or explicitly send messages to learners that they all are at the same stage of understanding and have nothing to bring to the learning experience.
- Teachers may spend a disproportionate amount of time teaching content that does not need to be taught or, at the very least, should be given less focus.
- The learning is pitched at one level rather than at a level where individual needs are catered to.
- The teachers' instructions are fixed, and they show little flexibility in their approaches to teaching and learning.
- There is little opportunity to be responsive to the particular needs of the learner.
- The learner is viewed as an empty container that needs to be filled up.
- Adjustments to instruction and curriculum made on the basis of formal or informal assessment are not evident.
- There may be lower levels of students on task and increased incidents of misbehavior.

When Consideration of Existing Knowledge Is Evident

A learning culture where existing knowledge is mindfully considered and applied may show evidence of:

- High levels of learning engagement and high-quality task completion
- Teachers who demonstrate an ability to adjust curriculum, instruction, and assessment based on information they have from the learner
- Students who are more engaged and spend greater amounts of time in the areas where they need to deepen their understanding
- Teachers who show greater effort to differentiate the content, process, or task for students based on what students have already demonstrated that they know
- Teachers who are more likely to connect the learning to the lifeworlds of their students through accessing their existing knowledge

- Teachers who spend a greater proportion of time checking for understanding and helping to make connections for the learner
- Mutual respect between teachers and learners that is evident through the way they speak with one another and the support teachers provide

Think and Reflect

1. How might you formatively assess your students' existing knowledge?
2. What are some strategies you can employ to find out what students already know?
3. In what ways might you change your approach to assessment, curriculum, or instruction based on information you get from your students?
4. How might you use existing knowledge, and how might it impact your curriculum-planning process?
5. How could you support your students to link new information with existing knowledge?
6. What might you do when it becomes apparent that your students already know what you have planned?

Supporting Ideas and Research

The following resources provide additional information and ideas you can use to further develop your concept of existing knowledge.

Costa, A. L., & Kallick, B. (Eds.) (2008). *Learning and leading with habits of mind: 16 essential characteristics for success*. Alexandria, VA: Association for Supervision and Curriculum Development. Costa and Kallick discuss the habit of mind *applying past knowledge to new situations* and provide a means of assessing students' development in this area.

Fisher, D., & Frey, N. (2014). *Checking for understanding: Formative assessment techniques for your classroom* (2nd ed.). Alexandria, VA: Association for Supervision and Curriculum Development. Fisher and Frey outline a variety of strategies to ensure teachers understand the power of formative assessment practices in ascertaining how to respond to students at the point of need.

Sousa, D. A. (2017). *How the brain learns* (5th ed.). Thousand Oaks, CA: Corwin Press. Sousa proposes how the brain works in retrieving information from the long-term memory and ways in which teachers can support this happening successfully.

Wiggins, G., & McTighe, J. (2005). *Understanding by design* (Expanded 2nd ed.). Alexandria, VA: Association for Supervision and Curriculum Development. Wiggins and McTighe outline a design process that supports learning for understanding. An integral aspect of their work is honoring student understanding in constructing the learning planning process. The understanding-by-design process supports this and many of the other learning considerations outlined in this book.

Appendix

This appendix supports chapter 7.

Our Class Learning Plan 2020

By J. S. Beadle

Everyone in our year helped to write these guidelines for our classroom.

These guidelines will help us to follow our school rules.

They will also help us to become successful learners.

As a member of the class, I will use these guidelines to help me become a terrific learner during 2020.

Our Class Motto

In 2B, we work our best.

As a team, we achieve success.

Everyone, each girl and boy,
learns and helps and cares with joy!

In our classroom, safety means …

- We will walk in the classroom
- We will sit on our chair, keeping its four legs on the floor
- We will hold and use scissors sensibly
- We will pass things to each other carefully
- We will play and work sensibly, by the rules
- We will push in our chair when we leave our table

In our classroom, learning means …

- We will work quietly

- We will listen and watch carefully

- We will use the keys to success to help us with our work

- We will ask the teacher to help if we don't understand

- We will help each other to learn

In our classroom, respect means …

- We will use put-ups, not put-downs

- We will accept that others might have different ideas

- We will treat others the way we would like to be treated

- We will take care of school property

- We will take care of our own and others' belongings

Teachers as Architects of Learning © 2020 Solution Tree Press and Hawker Brownlow Education
SolutionTree.com • Visit **go.SolutionTree.com/instruction** to download this free reproducible.

In our classroom, responsibility means …

- We will follow our school rules
- We will tell the truth
- We will make sensible choices

In our classroom, courtesy means …

- We will help each other
- We will use good manners
- We will put up our hands when we want to speak
- We will listen to others' ideas
- We will use eye contact when we are speaking with someone

Letter to Parents (adapted for publication)

The Learning Perspective
Our Philosophy

Our philosophy on education is really quite simple. Any person is going to learn enthusiastically, independently, and therefore successfully if he or she is in an environment that:

- Accepts and celebrates individual differences
- Is based on mutual respect
- Fosters and values the development of self-esteem
- Encourages the individual to take responsibility for his or her own actions and choices
- Understands and accepts that everybody has strengths and weaknesses
- Gives meaningful, honest, and constructive feedback
- Promotes teamwork, cooperation, and a positive approach to solving problems
- Allows students to be supportive of one another
- Invites students to share a laugh and a sense of humor
- Encourages students to make and accept mistakes and see them as vitally important in developing new knowledge
- Encourages risk taking both academically and socially
- Enables the student to feel safe and valued as an individual

Why a learning plan?

For students to feel as though they have a say in what happens in the classroom, one thing has to happen: *they have to have a say!* This learning plan is about everyone having ownership over our classroom environment so students are more likely to implement the conditions we've discussed. A happy student and teacher will lead to a happy classroom environment. This is absolutely essential in ensuring meaningful and effective learning can take place.

Why give it to parents?

Both personal and professional experience and a bit of common sense have enabled us to see just how important parents' attitudes are toward the success of their children as students. Parents, who understand what is happening in their children's education and therefore display an informed, positive, and active interest, are providing their children with an opportunity to share an important part of their young lives—education. If you have any comments or queries or would just like a general chat about the way we manage behavior in our class, please contact us at school at any time to make an appointment.

Education is not only about academic achievement. It's equipping students with skills for lifelong learning.

Teachers as Architects of Learning © 2020 Solution Tree Press and Hawker Brownlow Education
SolutionTree.com • Visit **go.SolutionTree.com/instruction** to download this free reproducible.

Learning Plan

We are who we choose to be!

Learning Plan

A Message From Mr. Milsum and Mrs. Hannan

Our learning plan is one of the most important documents we have put together. All students were involved in developing the plan and together decided the values that underpin the way we learn and behave are:

- Learning
- Safety
- Enjoyment

We also support the 3 Rs of Talent High School:

- Respect for self
- Respect for others
- Responsibility for actions

We have discovered through creating the learning plan that we are individually responsible for our own learning and actions and therefore:

We are who we choose to be!

Learning Plan

We strive to cooperate successfully by:

- Asking people to join in respectfully

- Letting people play if they are just standing there

- Changing the rules so others can play

- Making decisions on what we want

- Combining each other's ideas to make a decision

- Lending people your stuff if they want to borrow it

- Speaking respectfully and clearly to others

- Looking at the bright side of anybody's ideas

- First saying what you do like, then what you don't like, about an idea

Learning Plan

Successful Cooperation

We deal with fights and arguments by:

- Talking about it calmly

- Trying to find a solution within the group

- Apologizing and trying to get along with each other

We make decisions in a group by:

- Respecting people who give suggestions and reasons

- Asking everyone in our group if they have an idea

- Knowing that if everyone agrees, we've made a good decision

We use sharing skills by:

- Sharing things that others might enjoy

- Taking turns and respecting other people's belongings

- Letting other people borrow our things

We suggest and persuade instead of bossing, by:

- Giving reasons for your idea

- Justifying if it is a good idea by giving good reasons why it is

- If the group doesn't agree with your idea, trying to think of another one

Learning Plan

Rights and Responsibilities

We have the responsibility to:

- Clean up after ourselves

- Respect ourselves and others

- Care for ourselves and others

- Try our best and work when asked

- Work cooperatively and share materials

- Be honest

- Accept consequences

We have the right to:

- Feel safe in the classroom

- Be treated with respect and fairly

- Learn, work, and play in a supportive environment

- Ask questions and be listened to

- Have our own opinion

- Try something new and learn through making mistakes

Learning Plan

Respect

We treat each other with respect by:

- Being the first to show respect

- Making everyone feel welcome

- Caring for each other and equipment

- Being well mannered

- Including others

- Treating others the way we would like to be treated

- Reflecting the no-put-down-zone mission

- Listening to others

- Helping people and encouraging

- Seeking to understand, as well as be understood

Learning Plan

To increase our levels of thinking we use many strategies, including:

- De Bono's six thinking hats
- Gardner's multiple intelligences
- Thinker's keys
- Classroom contracts
- Classroom meetings
- Portfolios
- Self-assessment
- Developing criteria for self-assessment
- Negotiating the curriculum

In our grade level, our efforts toward learning are recognized through:

- Peer recognition
- Classroom thermometer
- Teacher feedback
- Table points
- Lottery tickets

Learning Plan

Class Message

We welcome all visitors to our classroom and accept the consequences of good and poor choices.

We support our learning plan because it helps us learn to the best of our ability, allows us to enjoy our class, and keeps us safe.

Learning Plan

Mottos That Didn't Make the Final Cut

1. Hannan's classroom: where loopy children are only just the beginning

2. The students are smarter here

3. We are on the very brink of becoming masters of the think

4. Finger-licking thinkers

5. Two, four, six, eight—learning fast is our fate

6. Attitudes are contagious; is yours worth catching?

7. And we're climbing the stairway to thinking …

Learning Plan

Classroom Journal

(Please add any comments about your experiences with our class here.)

Learning Plan

Classroom Journal

(Please add any comments about your experiences with our class here.)

References and Resources

Ainsworth, L. (2004). *Power standards: Identifying the standards that matter the most.* Englewood, CO: Advanced Learning Press.

Ainsworth, L., & Viegut, D. (2008). *Common formative assessments: How to connect standards-based instruction and assessment.* Melbourne, Australia: Hawker Brownlow Education.

Archer, A. L., & Hughes, C. A. (2011). *Explicit instruction: Effective and efficient teaching.* New York: Guilford Press.

Assessment Reform Group. (1999). *Assessment for learning: Beyond the black box.* Cambridge: Cambridge University, School of Education.

Ausubel, D. P., Novak, J. D., & Hanesian, H. (1978). *Educational psychology: A cognitive view* (2nd ed.). New York: Holt, Rinehart & Winston.

Bandura, A. (1997). *Self-efficacy.* New York: W. H. Freeman.

Barnett, B. G., O'Mahony, G. R., & Matthews, R. J. (2004). *Reflective practice: The cornerstone for school improvement.* Melbourne, Australia: Hawker Brownlow Education.

Berk, L. E., & Winsler, A. (1995). Scaffolding children's learning: Vygotsky and early childhood education. *NAEYC Research Into Practice*, Vol. 7.

Black, P., & Wiliam, D. (2004). *Inside the black box: Raising standards through classroom assessment.* London: King's College.

Bloom, B. S., Engelhart, M. D., Furst, E. J., Hill, W. H., & Krathwohl, D. R. (Eds). (1956). *Taxonomy of educational objectives.* New York: Longmans, Green.

Boud, D. J. (1986). *Implementing student self-assessment.* Kensington, Australia: Higher Education Research and Development Society of Australasia.

Boud, D. J. (1995). *Enhancing learning through self-assessment.* London: Kogan Page.

Bower, G. H., & Hilgard, E. R. (1981). *Theories of learning* (5th ed.). Englewood Cliffs, NJ: Prentice-Hall.

Boyles, N. N. (2007). *Hands-on literacy coaching.* Gainesville, FL: Maupin House.

Bransford, J. D., Brown, A. L., & Cocking, R. R. (2000). *How people learn: Brain, mind, experience, and school* (Expanded ed.). Washington, DC: National Academies Press.

Bruner, J. S. (1990). *Acts of meaning*. Cambridge, MA: Harvard University Press.

Bruner, J. S. (2009). *Actual minds, possible worlds*. Cambridge, MA: Harvard University Press.

Buffum, A., Mattos, M., & Weber, C. (2009). *Pyramid response to intervention*. Bloomington, IN: Solution Tree Press.

Cambourne, B. (1988). *The whole story: Natural learning and the acquisition of literacy in the classroom*. Jefferson City, MO: Scholastic Inc.

Campbell, L., & Campbell, B. (2009). *Mindful learning: 101 proven strategies for student and teacher success* (2nd ed.). Thousand Oaks, CA: Corwin Press.

Carlson, N. R. (2013). *Physiology of behavior*. Boston: Pearson.

Chappuis, J. (2009). *Seven strategies of assessment for learning*. Melbourne, Australia: Hawker Brownlow Education.

City, E. A., Elmore, R. F., Fiarman, S. E., & Teitel, L. (2009). *Instructional rounds in education*. Cambridge, MA: Harvard Education Press.

Clarke, S. (2001). *Unlocking formative assessment*. London: Hodder Education.

Costa, A. L., & Garmston, R. J. (2006). *Cognitive coaching: A foundation for renaissance in schools*. Melbourne, Australia: Hawker Brownlow Education.

Costa, A. L., Garmston, R. J., Ellison, J., & Hayes, C. (2016). *Cognitive coaching foundation seminar: Learning guide*. Melbourne, Australia: Hawker Brownlow Education.

Costa, A. L., Garmston, R. J., & Zimmerman, D. P. (2014). *Cognitive capital: Investing in teacher quality*. New York: Teachers College Press.

Costa, A. L., & Kallick, B. (2000a). *Habits of mind: Assessing and reporting* (Vol. 3). Melbourne, Australia: Hawker Brownlow Education.

Costa, A. L., & Kallick, B. (2000b). *Habits of mind: Discovering and exploring* (Vol. 1). Melbourne, Australia: Hawker Brownlow Education.

Costa, A. L., & Kallick, B. (2004). *Habits of mind: A developmental series: Activating and engaging habits of mind*. Melbourne, Australia: Hawker Brownlow Education.

Costa, A. L., & Kallick. B. (2008). *Learning and leading with habits of mind: 16 essential characteristics for success*. Alexandria, VA: Association for Supervision and Curriculum Development.

Covey, S. R. (1989). *The seven habits of highly effective people*. New York: Simon and Schuster..

Csikszentmihalyi, M. (1997). *Finding flow: The psychology of engagement with everyday life*. New York: Basic Books.

Danielson, C. (2007). *Enhancing professional practice: A framework for teaching* (2nd ed.). Alexandria, VA: Association for Supervision and Curriculum Development.

de Bono, E. (2009). *Six thinking hats*. London: Penguin Books.

Dewey, J. (1997). *Experience and education*. New York: Free Press.

Dewey, J. (2004). *Democracy and education*. Mineola, NY: Dover.

Dick, W., Carey, L., & Carey, J. O. (2009). *The systematic design of instruction* (7th ed.). Upper Saddle River, NJ: Pearson.

Dinham, S., Ingvarson, L., & Kleinhenz, E. (2008). Investing in teacher quality: Doing what matters most. In *Teaching talent: The best teachers for australia's classrooms* (pp. 5–53). Melbourne, Australia: Business Council of Australia.

Doidge, N. (2010). *The brain that changes itself*. Melbourne, Australia: Scribe.

DuFour, R., DuFour, R., & Eaker, R. (2008). *Revisiting Professional Learning Communities at Work: New insights for improving schools*. Bloomington, IN: Solution Tree Press.

DuFour, R., DuFour, R., Eaker, R., Many, T. W., & Mattos, M. (2016). *Learning by doing: A handbook for Professional Learning Communities at Work* (3rd ed.). Bloomington, IN: Solution Tree Press.

DuFour, R., DuFour, R., Eaker, R., Many, T., Mattos, M., Grift, G., & Sloper, C. (2017). *Learning by doing: A handbook for Professional Learning Communities at Work* (Revised Australian ed.). Melbourne, Australia: Hawker Brownlow Education.

Ellum, L., & Longmuir, F. (2013). *A different journey*. Melbourne, Australia: Bayside and Glen Eira Kingston Local Learning and Employment Network.

Erickson, L., & Tomlinson, C. A. (2007). *Concept-based curriculum and instruction for the thinking classroom*. Melbourne, Australia: Hawker Brownlow Education.

Ericsson, K. A., Krampe, R. T., & Tesch-Römer, C. (1993). The role of deliberate practice in the acquisition of expert performance. *Psychological Review*, *100*(3), 363–406.

Ericsson, K. A., Roring, R. W., & Nandagopal, K. (2007). Giftedness and evidence for reproducibly superior performance: An account based on the expert performance framework. *High Ability Studies*, *18*(1), 3–56.

Fisher, D., & Frey, N. (2015). *Checking for understanding: Formative assessment techniques for your classroom* (2nd ed.). Melbourne, Australia: Hawker Brownlow Education.

Fogarty, R. J. (2009). *Brain-compatible classrooms* (3rd ed.). Thousand Oaks, CA: Corwin Press.

Fogarty, R. J., & Pete, B. M. (2004). *A look at transfer: Seven strategies that work*. Thousand Oaks, CA: Corwin Press.

Gagné, R. M. (1985). *The conditions of learning and theory of instruction* (4th ed.). New York: Holt, Rinehart & Winston.

Gagné, R. M., Briggs, L. J., & Wager, W. W. (1992). *Principles of instructional design* (4th ed.). Fort Worth, TX: HBJ College.

Glasser, W. (2010). *Quality school teacher RI*. New York: HarperCollins.

Grift, G. (2007a). *Mulberry Hill cluster: Teaching and learning together curriculum planning review*. Melbourne, Australia: Department of Education and Early Childhood Training.

Grift, G. (2007b). *The ANSN curriculum planning hub*. www.nsn.net.au/sites/default/files/articles/ANSN_Snapshot_2_2008_web.pdf.

Grift, G. (2009). Beyond four walls: Curriculum design for authentic learning. *Teacher, 2009*(204), 6–9.

Grift, G., & Satchwell, J. (2007). *Assessing the whole child: Creating powerful portfolios and student led conferences*. Melbourne, Australia: Hawker Brownlow Education.

Hale, J. (2008). *A guide to curriculum mapping: Planning, implementing and sustaining the process*. Melbourne, Australia: Hawker Brownlow Education.

Hanover Research. (2012). *High expectations and student success*, Hanover Research Report for Springfield District.

Harpaz, Y., & Lefstein, A. (2000). Communities of thinking. *Educational Leadership, 58*(3), 54–57.

Hattam, R., & Bills, A. (2007). *Toward theorising the pedagogical challenge: A presentation to the Australian National Schools Network.* University of South Australia: Connecting Lives and Learning Project.

Hattie, J. A. (2003). *Teachers make a difference, What is the research evidence?* Melbourne, Australia: Australian Council of Educational Research Conference Archive.

Hattie, J. A. (2009). *Visible learning: A synthesis of over 800 meta-analyses relating to achievement.* London: Routledge.

Hill, P. W. (2003). *How to teach better: Pedagogy for deep learning.* Australia: Curriculum Corporation Conference.

Hoover, J. D., Giambatista, R. C., & Belkin, L. Y. (2012). Eyes on, hands on: Vicarious observational learning as an enhancement of direct experience. *Academy of Management Learning & Education, 11*(4), 591–608.

Hunter, M. (1994). *Mastery teaching.* Thousand Oaks, CA: Corwin Press.

Jacobs, H. H. (Ed.). (2010). *Curriculum 21: Essential education for a changing world.* Alexandria, VA: Association for Supervision and Curriculum Development.

Johnson, B., & Reid, A. (1999). *Contesting the curriculum.* Katoomba, Australia: Social Science Press.

Kemmis, S., Cole, P., & Suggett, D. (1983). *Orientations to curriculum and transition: Towards the socially-critical school.* Melbourne, Australia: Victorian Institute of Secondary Education.

Kolb, D. A. (1984). *Experiential learning: Experience as the source of learning and development.* Englewood Cliffs, NJ: Prentice-Hall.

Kuncel, N. R., Credé, M., & Thomas, L. L. (2005). The validity of self-reported grade point averages, class ranks, and test score: A meta-analysis and review of the literature. *Review of Educational Research, 75*(1), 63–82.

Labaree, D. F. (1997). *How to succeed in school without really learning: The credentials race in American education.* New Haven, CT: Yale University Press.

Levine, D. U., & Lezotte, L. W. (1990). *Unusually effective schools: A review and analysis of research and practice*. Madison, WI: The National Center for Effective Schools Research and Development.

Marzano, R. J. (2003). *What works in schools: Translating research into action*. Alexandria, VA: Association for Supervision and Curriculum Development.

Marzano, R. J. (2006). *A different kind of classroom: Teaching with dimensions of learning*. Melbourne, Australia: Hawker Brownlow Education.

Marzano, R. J. (2007). *The art and science of teaching: A comprehensive framework for effective instruction*. Melbourne, Australia: Hawker Brownlow Education.

Marzano, R. J. (2010). *On excellence in teaching*. Melbourne, Australia: Hawker Brownlow Education.

Marzano, R. J. (2012). *Becoming a reflective tacher*. Melbourne, Australia: Hawker Brownlow Education.

Marzano, R. J. (2017). *The new art and science of teaching*. Melbourne, Australia: Hawker Brownlow Education.

Marzano, R. J., & Marzano, J. S. (2010). The inner game of teaching. In R. J. Marzano (Ed.), *On excellence in teaching* (pp. 345–367). Bloomington, IN: Solution Tree Press.

Marzano, R. J., Pickering, D. J., & Heflebower, T. (2010). *The highly engaged classroom*. Melbourne, Australia: Hawker Brownlow Education.

Marzano, R. J., Pickering, D. J., & Pollock, J. E. (2001). *Classroom instruction that works: Research-based strategies for increasing student achievement*. Alexandria, VA: Association for Supervision and Curriculum Development.

Marzano, R. J., Waters, T., & McNulty, B. A. (2005). *School leadership that works: From research to results*. Alexandria, VA: Association for Supervision and Curriculum Development.

McDonald, B. (2012). *Gestalt effect of self-assessment*. West Indies: University of Trinidad and Tobago, O'Meara Campus.

McDonald, B., & Boud, D. (2003). The impact of self-assessment on achievement: The effects of self-assessment training on performance in external examinations. *Assessment in Education: Principles, Policy & Practice, 10*(2), 209–220.

Meltzer, L. J., Roditi, B. N., Steinberg, J. L., Rafter Biddle, K., Taber, S. E., Boyle Caron, K., & Kniffin, L. (2006). *Strategies for success: Classroom teaching techniques for students with learning differences* (2nd ed.). Austin, TX: PRO-ED.

Miller, N. E., & Dollard, J. (1941). *Social learning and imitation.* New Haven, CT: Yale University Press.

Moss, C. M., & Brookhart, S. M. (2009). *Advancing formative assessment in every classroom: A guide for instructional leaders.* Alexandria, VA: Association for Supervision and Curriculum Development.

National Governors Association Center for Best Practices & Council of Chief State School Officers. (2010a). *Common Core State Standards for English language arts and literacy in history/social studies, science, and technical subjects.* Washington, DC: Authors. Accessed at www.corestandards.org/assets/CCSSI_ELA%20Standards.pdf on April 7, 2020.

Nottingham, J. (2010). *Challenging learning.* Melbourne, Australia: Hawker Brownlow Education.

Ormrod, J. E. (2004). *Human learning* (4th ed.). Upper Saddle River, NJ: Merrill.

Ormrod, J. E. (2006). *Educational psychology: Developing learners* (5th ed.). Upper Saddle River, NJ: Pearson/Merrill Prentice Hall.

Otero, G., & Csoti, R., & Rothstadt, D. (2018). *Creating powerful learning relationships: A whole-school community approach* (2nd ed.). Melbourne, Australia: Hawker Brownlow Education.

Pavlov, I. P., & Anrep, G. V. (1927). *Conditioned reflexes.* London: Oxford University Press.

Perkins, D. (1992). *Smart schools: Better thinking and learning for every child.* New York: Free Press. Precis of "Generative and Fragile Knowledge" statement taken from presentation by Di Peck (Department of Education and Early Childhood, Victoria) referencing David Perkins.

Perkins, D. (1998). What is understanding? In M. S. Wiske (Ed.), *Teaching for understanding: Linking research with practice* (pp. 39–57). San Francisco: Jossey-Bass.

Perkins, D., & Blythe. T. (1994). Putting understanding up front. *Educational Leadership, 51*(5), 4–7.

Perls, F. S. (1973). *The Gestalt approach & eye witness to therapy.* Ben Lomond, CA: Science & Behavior Books.

Pete, B. M., & Fogarty, R. J. (2003). *Twelve brain principles that make a difference.* Thousand Oaks, CA: Corwin Press.

Piaget, J., & Vonèche, J. (2007). *The child's conception of the world*. Langham, MD: Rowman & Littlefield.

Popham, W. J. (2005). *Classroom assessment: What teachers need to know* (4th ed.). Boston: Pearson/Allyn and Bacon.

Prosser, B. Lucas, W., & Reid, A. (2010). *Connecting lives and learning: Renewing pedagogy in the middle years*. Kent Town, Australia: Wakefield Press.

Rieger, E. (2012). *Abnormal psychology: Leading researcher perspectives*. Sydney, Australia: McGraw-Hill Australia.

Rogers, C. R. (1951). *Client-centered therapy, its current practice, implications, and theory*. Boston: Houghton Mifflin.

Rosenshine, B. (1987). Explicit teaching and teacher training. *Journal of Teacher Education*, *38*(3), 34–36.

Rotter, J. B. (1982). *The development and applications of social learning theory: Selected papers*. New York: Praeger.

Rowe, M. B. (1974). Relation of wait-time and rewards to the development of language, logic, and fate control: Part II—Rewards. *Journal of Research in Science Teaching*, *11*(4), 291–308.

Rutherford, P. (2002). *Why didn't I learn this in college?* Alexandria, VA: Just ASK.

Salovey, P., & Mayer, J. D. (1990). Emotional intelligence. *Imagination, Cognition and Personality*, *9*(3), 185–211.

Schlechty, P. C. (2002). *Working on the work : An action plan for teachers, principals, and superintendents*. San Francisco: Jossey-Bass.

Schön, D. A. (1983). *The reflective practitioner: How professionals think in action*. New York: Basic Books.

Schön, D. A. (1987). *Educating the reflective practitioner: Toward a new design for teaching and learning in the professions*. San Francisco: Jossey-Bass.

Schrage, M. (2000). *Serious play: How the world's best companies simulate to innovate*. Boston: Harvard Business School Press.

Schreck, M. K. (2011). *You've got to reach them to teach them: Hard facts about the soft skills of student engagement*. Melbourne, Australia: Hawker Brownlow Education.

Seaton, A. (2002). Reforming the hidden curriculum: The key abilities model and the four curricular forms. *Curriculum Perspectives, 22*(1), 9–15.

Seligman, M. E. P. (1995). *The optimistic child*. Sydney, Australia: Random House.

Seligman, M. E. P. (2011). *Flourish*. London: Nicholas Brealey.

Sempowicz, T., & Hudson, P. (2011). Analysing mentoring dialogues for developing a preservice teacher's classroom management practices. *Australian Journal of Teacher Education*, *36*(8), 1–16.

Skinner, B. F. (1968). *The technology of teaching*. New York: Appleton-Century-Crofts.

Skinner, B. F., & Ferster, C. B. (1997). *Schedules of reinforcement*. Acton, MA: Copley Publishing Group.

Sousa, D. A. (2006). *How the brain learns*. Melbourne, Australia: Hawker Brownlow Education.

Sousa, D. A., & Tomlinson, C. A. (2018). *Differentiation and the brain: How neuroscience supports the learner-friendly classroom* (2nd ed.). Bloomington, IN: Solution Tree Press.

Stiggins, R. (2007). Assessment through the student's eyes. *Educational Leadership*, *64*(8), 22–26.

Stiggins, R., Arter, A., Chappuis, J., & Chappuis, S. (2007). *Classroom assessment for student learning: Doing it right—using it well*. Upper Saddle River, NJ: Pearson.

Stone Wiske, M. (Ed.). (1998). *Teaching for understanding: Linking research with practice*. San Francisco: Jossey-Bass.

Tomlinson, C. A. (2004). *Fulfilling the promise of the differentiated classroom*. Melbourne, Australia: Hawker Brownlow Education.

Udelhofen, S. (2005). *Keys to curriculum mapping: Strategies and tools to make it work*. Thousand Oaks, CA: Corwin Press.

Ulman, J. D., & Sulzer-Azaroff, B. (1975). Multielement baseline design in educational research In E. Ramp & G. Semb (Eds.), *Behavior analysis: Areas of research and application* (pp. 377–391). Englewood Cliffs, NJ: Prentice-Hall.

Varela, F. J., Thompson, E., & Rosch, E. (1991). *The embodied mind: Cognitive science and human experience*. Cambridge, MA: MIT Press.

von Glasersfeld, E. (2007). *Key works in radical constructivism*. Rotterdam: Sense.

Vygotsky, L. S. (2012). *Thought and language* (Revised and expanded ed.). Cambridge, MA: MIT Press.

Weber, C., Hierck, T., & Larson, G. (2016). *Collaborative systems of support: Learning for all*. Melbourne, Australia: Hawker Brownlow Education.

Wiggins, G., & McTighe, J. (2005). *Understanding by design* (2nd ed.). Melbourne, Australia: Hawker Brownlow Education.

Wiliam, D. (2018). *Embedded formative assessment* (2nd ed.). Bloomington, IN: Solution Tree Press.

Willis, J. (2008). *How your child learns best*. Naperville, IL: Sourcebooks.

Index

A

accountability, 90
achievement
    desire and, 105
    expectations and, 85–86
    lifeworlds and, 97
    self-assessment and, 44–45
    support/safety and, 73, 74
Ainsworth, L., 79
Animal Farm (Orwell), 103–104
anxiety, 2, 67, 77, 81, 113, 115
Assessing the Whole Child (Grift & Satchwell), 67
assessment
    end-of-year, 72–73
    expectations and, 89, 90
    formative, 7
    learner-oriented and teacher-oriented,
        35–36
    with/without observing and listening, 51–52
    self-, 18–19, 21, 35–46
    support/safety and, 72
    time for, 82, 83
Assessment Reform Group, 7
attendance, 105
attention. *See also engagement*
    focusing, 111
    generating, 56, 58
Australian National Schools Network, 2–3, 78
authentic audiences, 101–102

B

Baden-Powell, R., 47
behavior problems
    desire and, 104–105
    modeling/exemplars and, 65
    observing/listening and, 49
    questioning and, 32, 33
    resources and, 113
    self-assessment and, 44
    support/safety and, 74
behavioral learning support, 70
behaviorist learning theory, 9–12, 56, 62
Black, P., 31–32
Blair, G. R., 109
Bloom, B., 28
Blythe, T., 6, 8, 14
Boud, D. J., 35
Boyles, N., 55
bullying, 74

C

Campbell, B., 118
Campbell, L., 118
cognitive learning support, 69
cognitivist learning theory, 9–12
collaborative relationships, 37–38, 70
Common Core State Standards Initiative, 22–23
communication, 95, 111–113
concepts, key, 87–88
confidence, 65
connectedness, 101, 113
Connecting Lives to Learning Project, 93
consciousness of teaching, 15–16
consolidation of learning, 111
constructivist learning theory, 9–12, 79–80
constructs, 13, 17–23
    definition of, 18
    desire, 20–21, 22, 99–107
    existing knowledge, 21, 22, 117–122
    expectations, 20, 22, 85–91
    explicit instruction, 19, 21, 55–60
    how to use this book and, 23–25
    lifeworlds, 20, 22, 93–98
    modeling and exemplars, 19, 22, 61–66

observing and listening, 19, 21, 47–53
questioning, 18, 21, 27–34
resources, 21, 22, 109–115
self-assessment, 18–19, 21, 35–46
support and safety, 19–20, 22, 67–75
time, 20, 22, 77–84
content, focus on learning vs. teaching, 3
continuums, learning, 39
cortisol, 115
Costa, A., 16
creative thinking, 8
Credé, M., 35, 37
critical thinking, 8
Csikszentmihalyi, M., 100
Csoti, R., 94
culture. *See also safety*
collaborative learning, 38–42
expectations in, 86–91
habits of mind and, 8
learning-centered, 3
resources and, 113, 114
safe and supportive, 19–20, 22, 29
self-assessment and, 37–38
of support and safety, 19–20, 22, 67–75
curriculum development, 4

D

data collection, 48–49
de Bono, E., 69
decision making
student empowerment for, 37, 38
delight, 94–95
demonstration of learning, 56–57, 59
desire, 20–21, 22, 99–107
definition of, 99
learning environment with/without, 104–105
modeling/exemplars and, 65
rationale for, 99–100
research on, 106–107
resources and, 113
scenarios on, 103–104

self-assessment and, 44–45
strategies, 100–102
thinking/reflecting on, 106
differentiating instruction, 77
existing knowledge and, 121
self-assessment and, 43
time for, 82–83
diverse learners, 22
existing knowledge and, 121
expectations and, 85–91
self-assessment and, 37
dropout rates, 63–64
DuFour, R., 5, 8, 78
Dunstan, S., 49–51
duplication, 80

E

Eaker, R., 5, 8, 78
educational change, 5–12
Einstein, A., 99
empathy, 47, 48
empowerment, 37, 38, 72
engagement. *See also desire*
existing knowledge and, 121
expectations and, 90
learning continuums and, 39
lifeworlds and, 95, 97
self-assessment and, 37–38, 43, 44–45
evidence, key, 87–88
examinations, end-of-year, 72–73
exemplars, 19, 22, 61–66
definition of, 61
explicit instruction and, 55
rationale for, 61–62
research on, 66
scenarios on, 63–64
strategies, 62–63
thinking/reflecting on, 66
existing knowledge, 21, 22, 32, 33, 117–122
definition of, 117–122
expectations and, 89–90

learning environment with/without, 121–122
with/without observing and listening, 51–52
questioning and, 32, 33
rationale for, 117–118
research on, 122
scenarios on, 119–120
strategies, 118–119
thinking/reflecting on, 122
expectations, 20, 22, 85–91
definition of, 85
learning environment with/without, 89–90
minority groups and, 37
rationale for, 85–86
research on, 91
scenarios on, 88–89
self-assessment and, 37
strategies, 87–88
support/safety and, 71, 74
thinking/reflecting on, 91
expertise, 94
explicit instruction, 19, 21, 23, 55–60
definition of, 55
learning environment with/without, 59–60
rationale for, 55–56
research on, 60
scenarios on, 57–59
strategies, 56–57
thinking/reflecting on, 60

F

feedback, 21
modeling/exemplars for, 62
self-assessment and, 35–46
strategies for, 38–42
support with, 70, 71
time for, 80
Finding Flow: The Psychology of Engagement With Everyday Life (Csikszentmihalyi), 100
flexibility, 79–80, 121
flow states, 100

focus
on learning, 2–4
time and, 78
on what is valued, 4
fraction lunch box, 82
fractions, 81–82
fragile knowledge, 14–15
Friesen, C., 16
frustration, 44–45, 65, 105
fun, 71, 95, 102, 105

G

Garmston, R. J., 16
generative knowledge, 14–15, 28, 79
goals, 70
learning maps for, 40, 41
self-assessment and, 44–45
graphic organizers, 69
Grift, G., 14, 67
groups, cooperative, 62

H

habits of mind, 8
Hanover Research, 86
Hattie, J. A., 4, 35, 37, 77, 80
Herbert, F., 77
hit-and-hope approach to teaching, 83

I

imitation, 62
independent learning, 113, 114
independent study habits, 31–32
inquiry units, 42–43
integrated learning, 79, 101
International Baccalaureate, 86

K

Kazantzakis, N., 67
key concepts, 87

key knowledge, 87
knowledge
    Bloom's taxonomy of, 28
    existing, 21, 22, 117–122
    generative, 28, 79
    generative vs. fragile, 14–15, 28
    key, 87
    prior, 21, 22, 32, 33
Kuncel, N. R., 35, 37

L

learning
    activating successful student, 14–15
    consolidation of, 111
    constructs, 13, 17–23
    demonstrating, 56, 59
    diverse learners and, 22
    focusing on, 2–4, 78
    independent, 113, 114
    integrated, 79
    memorization of, 56, 59
    modalities, 62
    observational, 62
    performance of, 111
    reflection and, 14, 16
    replicating, 56, 59
    shaping behavior and, 70
    student-centered, 2–3
    teaching practices and, 14
    teaching vs., 2
learning consolidation, 69
learning continuums, 39
learning environment
    with/without desire, 104–105
    with/without effective questioning, 32–33
    with/without existing knowledge, 121–122
    with/without expectations, 89–90
    with/without explicit instruction, 59–60
    with/without lifeworld connections, 97
    with/without modeling and exemplars, 65

    with/without observing and listening, 51–52
    playful, 102
    with/without resources, 113–115
    with/without self-assessment, 44–45
    with/without support and safety, 74
    support and safety in, 67–75
    with/without time consideration, 82–83
learning experience, 14, 24–25
learning maps, 40, 41
learning plans, 123–138
learning portfolios, 49
learning theory, 9–12
legal studies, 119–120
Levine, D. U., 87
Lezotte, L. W., 87
lifeworlds, 20, 22, 93–98
    definition of, 93
    existing knowledge and, 121
    learning environment with/without, 97
    rationale for, 93–94
    research on, 98
    scenarios on, 95–96
    strategies, 94–95
    thinking/reflecting on, 98
listening, 19, 21, 47–53
    empathetic, 47
    learning environment with/without, 51–52
    rationale for, 47–48
    research on, 52–53
    scenarios on, 49–51
    strategies, 48–49
    thinking/reflecting on, 52
literature responses, 88–89
Lucas, W., 100

M

Marzano, R. J., 6–7, 8, 27, 47, 62, 109
MasterChef (TV show), 109–110
McDonald, B., 36–37
McKinnon, P., 1, 26

meeting schedules, 4
memorization, 56, 59, 80
mental models, 61
metacognitive abilities, 8, 69
minority group students, 37
modeling, 19, 22, 61–66
    definition of, 61
    explicit instruction and, 55
    instructional, 70
    learning environment with/without, 65
    observing/listening, 48
    rationale for, 61–62
    research on, 66
    scenarios on, 63–64
    strategies, 62–63
    thinking/reflecting on, 66
Mooney, P., 31–32
Mornington Inquiry Learning Centre, 86
Morrison, J., 93
motivation, 20–21. *See desire*

N

Neal, P., 85
neuroscience, 68, 99
The New Art and Science of Teaching
    (Marzano), 6–7
numeracy learning continuum, 39

O

Oakwood School, Victoria, Australia, 39
objectivist learning theory, 9–12
observational learning, 62
observing, 19, 21, 47–53
    definition of, 47
    learning environment with/without, 51–52
    rationale for, 47–48
    research on, 52–53
    scenarios on, 49–51
    strategies, 48–49
    thinking/reflecting on, 52

Orwell, G., 103–104
Otero, G., 94

P

peer teaching, 63, 71
performance of learning, 111
Perkins, D., 6, 8, 14
persuasive writing, 57–59
physical environment, 71
planning, 24–25, 63, 79. *See also time*
PLC at Work, 5–6
PowerPoint, 119–120
power standards, 79
practice, 79, 111
pretesting, 36
prior knowledge. See existing knowledge
problem solving, 71
procrastination, 104
professional learning communities (PLCs), 5–6
Project Zero, 17
Prosser, B., 100
purpose, in questioning, 28

Q

questioning, 18, 21, 23, 27–34
    to challenge traditional beliefs, 4
    definition of, 27
    dos and don'ts, 29–30
    existing knowledge and, 120
    intention in, 27–28
    with/without observing and listening, 51, 52
    rationale for, 27–28
    research/support on, 34
    scenarios on, 31–32
    strategies for, 28–30
    for structural support, 70
    support/safety and, 74
    tone/intonation in, 29, 33
    wait time and, 80, 82

R

racism teaching units, 49–51
reflection, 14, 16
    constructs for, 22
    on desire, 106
    on existing knowledge, 122
    on expectations, 91
    learning consolidation and, 69
    on lifeworlds, 98
    observing/listening and, 48
    on questioning, 34
    resistance to, 40, 42
    on resources, 115
    for self-assessment, 40, 42
    on self-assessment, 45
    self-assessment and, 21, 35–46
    on support and safety, 75
    on time, 83
    time for, 79–80, 82
Reid, A., 100
reinforcement, 70
replication of learning, 56, 59, 80
research, 11
    on desire, 106–107
    on existing knowledge, 122
    on expectations, 91
    on explicit instruction, 60
    on lifeworlds, 98
    on listening/observing, 52–53
    on modeling/exemplars, 66
    on the need for change, 5–12
    on questioning, 34
    on resources, 115
    on self-assessment, 45–46
    on support and safety, 75
    on time, 84
resistance, 40, 42
resources, 21, 22, 109–115
    definition of, 109
    learning environment with/without, 113–115
    rationale for, 109–110
    research on, 115
    scenarios on, 111–113
    strategies, 110–111
    thinking/reflecting on, 115
respect, 122
Rothstadt, D., 94

S

safety, 19–20, 22, 67–75
    definition of, 67
    learning environment with/without, 74
    questioning and, 29
    rationale for, 67–68
    research on, 75
    scenarios on, 72–73
    strategies, 69–72
    thinking/reflecting on, 75
Satchwell, J., 14, 67
scaffolding
    explicit instruction and, 55
    resources and, 111
    safety and, 67
    self-assessment skills, 38, 40, 42
self-assessment, 18–19, 21, 35–46
    data collection and, 48–49
    definition of, 35
    expectations and, 89, 90
    learning environment with/without, 44–45
    modeling/exemplars and, 65
    rationale for, 35–38
    research on, 45–46
    scenarios on, 42–43
    strategies, 38–42
    thinking/reflecting on, 45
self-efficacy, 37–38
self-regulated thinking, 8
shaping behavior, 70
skills, key, 87
Skinner, B. F., 56

slow schools movement, 78
social learning, 71
social learning theory, 9–12
social thinking, 62
Socrates, 117
Sousa, D. A., 48, 68, 99
strategies
    desire, 100–102
    exemplars and, 62–63
    existing knowledge, 118–119
    expectation, 87–88
    feedback, 38–42
    lifeworld, 94–95
    listening, 48–49
    modeling, 62–63
    observing, 48–49
    questioning, 28–30
    resources, 110–111
    safety, 69–72
    self-assessment, 38–42
stress, 114, 115
structural support, 70–72. *See also support*
student-centered learning, 2–3
success
    indicators of, 11
    models/exemplars for, 61, 63
    with/without observing and listening, 51–52
    resources and, 114–115
    self-assessment and, 37
support, 19–20, 22, 67–75
    definition of, 67
    for existing knowledge, 120
    learning environment with/without, 74
    questioning and, 29
    rationale for, 67–68
    research on, 75
    scenarios on, 72–73
    strategies, 69–72
    thinking/reflecting on, 75
sustainable environments, 95–96
Szymborska, W., 27

T
task completion, 113, 114
taxonomy of knowledge, 28
teaching
    based on learners' needs, 7
    hit-and-hope approach to, 83
    learning theories on, 9–12
    learning vs., 2
    new art and science of, 6–7
    peer, 63
    practices, learning and, 14, 15–16
    reflection on, 14, 16
    traditional beliefs about, 4
    for understanding, 6
    wisdom in, 12–13
Teaching for Understanding Project, 17
templates, self-assessment, 40, 42
textbooks, 120
think-alouds, 62
thinking hats, 69
Thomas, L. L., 35, 37
time, 20, 22, 77–84
    learning environment with/without, 82–83
    observing/listening and, 48
    rationale on, 77–78
    research on, 84
    scenarios on, 81–82
    for self-assessment, 38
    strategies, 79–80
    thinking/reflecting on, 83
time on task, 77–78
To Kill a Mockingbird (Lee), 49–51
Tomlinson, C. A., 48, 68, 99
tone/intonation, 29, 33
transference, 114

U
understanding, generating, 110

V

Van Doren, M., 35
Vygotsky, L., 118

W

wait time, 80, 82

Weber, C., 55
White, V., 78
Wiliam, D., 7, 8, 29–30
wisdom, teaching, 12–13
worked examples, 61–62